The Place of the Visual in Psychoanalytic Practice

The Place of the Visual in Psychoanalytic Practice: Image in the Countertransference explores the place of the visual image in psychoanalysis and psychotherapy, a still relatively unexplored topic in the psychoanalytic literature. Though 'talking therapies' are necessarily structured around the use of the spoken word, it can be difficult and at times misleading to explore the unconscious through speech alone.

This book examines how it may be further understood through recognising the presence of imagery as a form of non-verbal, but valuable, means of communication. Drawing on the work of Freud, Bion, Winnicott and Ogden, alongside other British and American contributions to this infrequently addressed subject, the book examines the connection between reverie, dream and daydream and explores the reservoirs of imagery of both client and therapist, focusing mainly on the therapists' visual countertransference.

Covering essential theory and a wealth of clinical material, *The Place of the Visual in Psychoanalytic Practice: Image in the Countertransference* is a rich yet accessible guide to both recognising and using visual imagery within the clinical setting for both psychoanalysts and psychotherapists.

Faye Carey is a psychoanalytic psychotherapist in private practice in London, UK and Chair of Training for the London Centre for Psychotherapy.

The Place of the Visual in Psychoanalytic Practice

Image in the Countertransference

Faye Carey

LONDON AND NEW YORK

First published 2018
by Routledge
2 Park Square, Milton Park, Abingdon, Oxon OX14 4RN

and by Routledge
711 Third Avenue, New York, NY 10017

Routledge is an imprint of the Taylor & Francis Group, an informa business

British Library Cataloguing-in-Publication Data
A catalogue record for this book is available from the British
Library

Library of Congress Cataloging-in-Publication Data
A catalog record for this book has been requested

ISBN: 978-1-138-30702-5 (hbk)
ISBN: 978-1-138-30705-6 (pbk)
ISBN: 978-1-315-14218-0 (ebk)

Typeset in Times New Roman
by Wearset Ltd, Boldon, Tyne and Wear

For Charles

Contents

Acknowledgements

This book has developed out of a doctoral thesis, entitled *Seeing Hearing* that I undertook at the University of Essex and my thanks go to my tutor, Nick Midgley and my supervisor, Karl Figlio for their support and guidance, and especially to my colleagues at the time who both challenged and stimulated the ideas as they developed. My gratitude goes also to the late James Fisher, who was my clinical supervisor when I began that undertaking some years ago, and whose conversation, thinking, ideas and comments have stayed with me while developing the original thesis into a book.

Finding material on the visual element in psychoanalytic work has been challenging, and I am grateful to PEP-Web and the many journals archived there to have such ready access to the accounts of clinical work that have been published by those authors, and their patients, who have generously provided us with insight into ways of working through direct experience.

My thanks to artist and poet Sophie Herxheimer for an enjoyable afternoon searching for, and finding, the cover image and to Charles Carey for helping me with visualising some of Freud's ideas ('Fort/Da' and 'Specimen Dream'). I am grateful to the Prado Museum for permission to print Velasquez's *Las Meninas*, and to Zac Carey for his assistance in getting the visual material into a presentable state.

My sincere thanks go to Kate Hawes for helping me to get started, to Charles Bath and Charlotte Taylor, and their colleagues at Routledge for their support, and to Anastasia Said, Hannah Riley and Allie Hargreaves at Wearset, for patiently shepherding me through the publication process.

Lastly, while the main emphasis in this book is on the visual experience of the therapist in the session, none of that would be possible without the stimulus and inspiration of the patients, my own and others, who have my deepest gratitude.

Faye Carey, 2017

Introduction

The technique, however, is a very simple one ...

(Freud 1912:111)

'What did you see?'

Well before the term 'psychoanalysis' was coined,[1] Freud described his 'small technical device'[2] for the treatment of hysteria. He would apply pressure to the patient's forehead, and assure him that during this time he would see before him 'a recollection in the form of a picture or will have it in his thoughts in the form of an idea occurring to him'. He would then remove his hand and ask, '"What did you see?" ...' (Freud 1893:270).

Freud soon abandoned this as a technique, and generally speaking, psychoanalysts now no longer normally touch, command or predict. But what has happened to the idea of the image, so central to this earliest description, for discovering the contents of the unconscious, both the *raison d'être* and the *sine qua non* of psychoanalytic therapies?

Experience soon taught Freud that these initially vivid images disintegrate as they are transformed into more structured and linear language,[3] a transformation that takes place in a different developmental register. 'What did you see?' recedes and is replaced, directly or implicitly, by 'What do you think?', or the more generic, 'What comes to mind?' The image – a more primitive (in the sense of 'earlier'), more compressed, layered, non-linear and compact construct – inevitably disappears as it is replaced by language, a later, more linear, more developmentally mature form of articulation. In the process of translating percepts, experiences, impressions and feelings into both written and spoken language, that is to say, the essential currency of psychoanalytic discourse, the visual inevitably recedes as the word advances.

As true as it is for the patient, this often subtle and unnoticed slippage from image to word is equally true for the therapist who is having, often rapidly, often unconsciously, to process such imagery as may arise in her[4] mind spontaneously in the session in order to articulate meaning both for herself (that is, translate from image-thought to speech-thought) as well as to prepare for sharing with the patient (a further, secondary, image-editing process), if the idea is to be communicated verbally as either observation or interpretation. This process usually happens so subtly, so imperceptibly, that – like the evanescing dream upon waking – it has disappeared from view, and receded into the unconscious before it has had time to register visually, or conceptually, in a meaningful way. Of course, the influence of the image may well remain, much as it would with a dream, but its disappearance from conscious awareness may nonetheless, result in the potential richness, depth and value of its content and meaning being diminished, or at times entirely lost, and therefore, either unavailable or less available, to the work of the therapy.

So, in processing ideas towards articulation – much as with interpreting dreams – we may paradoxically lose sight of the original source: the *ur* image that generates the relevant associations that have the capacity to reveal the inner workings of the mind, and thereby, lose its potential value as a tool of both insight and interpretation.

The dynamic disappearance of imagery

There is, however, something further to be understood with regard to the fugitive nature of imagery, something not merely circumstantial – that is to say, the unintended consequence of the inevitable dominance of spoken or written language in interpersonal communication – but also something more dynamic, to do with a form of resistance, that would help to account for such a relative lack of attention to the subject in the vast body of work relating to clinical practice. This disappearance of the visual may also be unconsciously strategic – an active, and at times, defensive process, arising from the challenge of the immediacy of the image and its associations.

Something of this process may be better understood by reference to dream processes, such as set out in Freud's description of the 'dream-work' (1900:277) wherein it is precisely the often oblique, apparently unrelated or detached nature of the imagery that mitigates against its becoming established in conscious awareness as relevant to the concerns in hand. Such images, like dreams, may dissipate into a sense of trivia, irrelevance or nonsense and – again like dreams – become 'forgotten'. But, as Freud showed, the imagery that has been processed through the dream-work is redolent of meaning that may be understood through attention and interpretation. So it may be with the visual material of the therapist's often ignored daydream that may undergo a parallel process, a type of 'daydream-work'. The daydream may thus, similarly be seen, clinically, as functioning as a form of crucible or container in which the material of the session is processed unconsciously, particularly where that material is difficult to metabolise, or is otherwise defended against, as I later discuss more fully.

A two-way process

The traffic between image and word, however, is not just one-way. For just as the word may defensively provide a refuge from the force or immediacy of the image, so the image may in its turn offer a retreat from explicit verbal articulation, if that is itself becoming uncomfortable. This reverse movement from language back to image may facilitate a distancing from articulation of difficult or complex thoughts and ideas, towards something more diffuse, vague and less immediately threatening or problematic: hence, the daydream. Within the analytic session, as well as the oscillation between the more vague and the more precise thinking that is characteristic of the therapist's state of 'freely-floating attention', there may also take place a similar oscillation between verbal and imagistic thinking, a two-way process that flows from one to the other and back again. Word retreats from image, and image yields to word, moving imperceptibly back-and-forth throughout the session. But what is recorded of this process is both scant and uneven: inevitably, the word dominates.

Imagery and daydream

The therapist's daydream overlaps with the function, in Bion's terms, of 'reverie', and here I would like to think about both the defensive and the creative aspects of the specifically visual nature of this phenomenon. Alongside the binary character of the image, functioning at times as retreat and at times as threat, as suggested above, there is a further duality that contributes to the discussion of imagery in the clinical setting: that of daydream and reverie. Whereas the term 'reverie' – that is the therapist's capacity for internal reflection while staying in affective touch with the patient – is recognised by many as a positive and valued, in fact essential, therapeutic tool, the term 'daydream', by contrast, is often employed to describe a more self-absorbed state, 'time out' from the concerns, uncertainties, internal conflicts, intensity or simply the 'not knowing' of the session, where the work in hand is being avoided or evaded. The 'daydream' is therefore, often regarded as something for which to chastise oneself, and 'come out of'.

It is this flow between word, image and daydream (or reverie), in both their passive and active forms that I want to follow here. Through tracking this process, both the incidental on the one hand and the dynamic on the other, I hope to demonstrate how pictures and words appear to hold each other in tension, a form of defensive-creative balance, with one providing a potential psychic retreat or refuge from the other when either threatens impingement, and how becoming more aware of this movement may benefit both the therapist's technique, and the progress of the therapy.

Pictures, words and pictures

It will be seen that the loss of the visual within psychoanalytic discourse and practice has a certain circularity about it: the therapist must necessarily use language to communicate thoughts, verbally to the patient and in writing, when sharing clinical experience professionally. Within the constraints of the session, as the image gives way to the word, these visual experiences are not often afforded much spoken or recorded space, and are therefore, rarely picked up as relevant within psychoanalytic discourse. As it mutates into written and spoken word, the image seems actually to get lost from the mind, and this further contributes to an impression that visualisation is inconsequential as a phenomenon, of scant clinical value. As imagery and visualisation are therefore less frequently the subject of common parlance within psychoanalytic literature, they are as a result regarded as less significant than may actually be the case, and remain dormant as aspects of both training and practice, with the result that the therapist continues to overlook the visual experience or devalue it as incidental or irrelevant. Put simply, little space has been made for this dimension.

However, it could also be seen as a form of scotomisation – a more dynamic oversight, that is a self-perpetuating condition, and an impression I wish to challenge since I regard its loss as detrimental to both psychoanalytic insight and therapeutic practice.

Mental imagery and the visual countertransference

To understand the role of the visual in this process more fully, as well as the conditions of its appearance, disappearance and reappearance, I will explore generally aspects of mental imagery as they are represented in the very language of the relevant narratives that descriptively evoke, or revive, the original images. These include details of objects, people, places and spaces, visual metaphor and simile, shape, colour, tone, rhythm, size, scale, proportion and other sensory descriptors such as gesture and movement as they appear in the material of the session, in dreams and daydreams, in the patient, as well as in the thoughts and countertransference experience of the therapist.

A particular question is, in the presence of the patient, whether speaking or silent, what – if anything – may the images that arise spontaneously in the therapist's mind (what I am calling the 'visual countertransference') say about the patient's internal world? How does the therapist 'see' what she or he hears – directly or indirectly – and then make sense of these images using those techniques of interpretation already familiar to us within clinical practice, especially with regard to dreams, that undeniably rich repository of imagery?

Reclaiming the visual

If, as I suggest, imaging and visualisation are significant elements of dimensional[5] awareness, having the potential to contribute to a more articulate and nuanced understanding of the psyche, then their relative neglect within psychoanalytic discourse raises questions. The immense importance attributed to dreams alone in classical psychoanalytic theory and practice is testament enough to the recognition of the visual element as a rich therapeutic resource.

I therefore, consider how the image in the session, at varying levels of consciousness, for both patient and therapist, may function both defensively (flight from verbal articulation), anxiously (a persistent image that is difficult to dislodge), but also creatively, whereby retreat to the daydream, in what appears at first sight to be a form of escape, may ultimately provide a space of reflection that may yield insight, in much the same way as is provided by the associative analysis of a dream. To explore this process further, I draw substantively on Freud's theory of dream construction (i.e. the 'dream-work') as a model for understanding that of the daydream (or what I paraphrase as 'daydream-work').

Alongside the dynamics of both the appearance and disappearance of the image, I attempt to evaluate that richness, and think about how to retrieve the place of the visual both theoretically and clinically. Ultimately, I argue for the recovery, and evaluation or re-evaluation of the visual component, through attending to the imagery that occurs in different contexts and at differing levels of consciousness, within the psychoanalytic session. I consider both how and, to some extent, why, we 'see what we hear', directly or indirectly, through noting the visual element of those processes in the therapist – free-floating attention, imagery, reverie and daydream – that are the counterpart of the patient's 'free association', enactments and dreams.

Chapter outline

In *Chapter 1 What is a mental image?* I introduce the idea of the 'mental image' as a form of visual representation that is held in mind in the absence of any material manifestation, be that a person, object, place, event, relationship (of persons or objects) or experience. It can be vague or detailed, static or fluid, seen in colour or monochrome, experienced as silent or with a sense of accompanying sound. Further, the images with which I am concerned here are more likely to be those that appear obliquely rather than in direct response to something that is being described in the moment. With regard to the clinical session, although both are significant, I am more concerned with the imagery that comes to the mind of the therapist than I am of the patient, as the object of this enquiry is to consider the use that the therapist might make of such imagery towards clinical understanding. A clinical example helps to illustrate the use of imagery in the session.

Chapter 2 Spatiality, dimensionality and the visual discusses the relationship between the development of dimensionality, or the idea of internal space, its role in emotional and psychological growth, and the capacity to visualise and imagine, since an image needs a space in which to live and, to some extent, to be framed. I draw here on Freud's many uses of spatial metaphor and its foundational contribution to psychoanalytic thought, as well as approaches from Kleinian, Post-Kleinian and Object Relations schools of thought including those of Melanie Klein (projection, position and oscillation), Esther Bick (surface and skin), Donald Winnicott (potential, transitional and overlapping space and movement) and the chief theoretical references, Wilfred Bion (containment) and Donald Meltzer (claustrum states and other writings on dimensionality). Further thoughts on the theme of dimensionality and its place in emotional development come from Milner, Money-Kyrle and Ogden. Clinical examples serve to illustrate the importance of this area of development as it relates to the growth of the capacity to form and to retain an image in the absence of the object.

Much of the emphasis here is on the phenomenon of imagery in the session as something that is largely, albeit unconsciously, co-constructed and is to some extent a consequence of projection. *Chapter 3 Unconscious communication: projection, projective identification, reverie and countertransference* lays the foundation for this aspect of the discussion by providing a review of the growth of ideas regarding projective processes, focusing mainly on the visual element, and this primarily within the countertransference experience. I outline the development of attitudes regarding the phenomenon of the countertransference and its evolution within psychoanalytic theory and practice, from Freud and Jung, through Klein and Segal, Heiman and Racker, Rosenfeld, Bion, Ogden, Bollas, Jacobs, Lasky and others whose work I feel helps to shed light on this particular aspect of the countertransference, that is, its visual form, even though it is not necessarily the subject specifically under study in those examples. I illustrate the concept with both pre-published and original clinical material.

In *Chapter 4 Considerations of representability: visualisation and image construction in reverie, dream and daydream* I turn to the central theme of image formation, beginning with early accounts of the nature of representation and representability, considering theories of how images form – particularly in the idiosyncratic, at times hypnogogic, context of the clinical setting. I consider the relationship between images and words, also in these unusual conditions, and draw on the work of a few American writers who, at different times and in a variety of contexts, paid attention to this area of experience, such as Warren, Isakower, Lewin and Horowitz, alongside others who expanded on and developed work in this field: the prevalence of imagery in the hypnogogic state.

My emphasis here is how that state may encourage such imagery in the therapist, a form of countertransference and I develop the key theme of the therapist's daydream, how it relates structurally to the sleeping dream, (or how the processes of the 'daydream-work' relate to those of the 'dream-work') that is similarly open to a parallel form of interpretation. I discuss the elements of condensation, compression, symbol, illusion and allusion, whether as dream, daydream or painting, and refer to Velasquez's *Las Meninas* on the one hand, and to Freud's 'Specimen Dream' on the other, as illustrations of the complex and layered nature of imagery. I conclude with aspects of Donald Meltzer's critique of Freud's dream theory.

In *Chapter 5 Dynamics of imagery* the emphasis is on the dynamic function of visualisation in the clinical encounter. On the one hand, this may be 'neutral', a spontaneous response, association or sequence of associations to the context of the session. However, more dynamically, image formation may serve as a retreat from something uncomfortable, providing a temporary refuge while the difficulty, hopefully, is processed. Even so, the imagery arising at such times, on reflection, may nonetheless inform the therapist's eventual understanding. By contrast, a further and converse, dynamic of visualisation is that the image can itself evoke uncomfortable associations, and the tendency then may be to find refuge in words. This oscillation, I suggest, is a common, though not always conscious, dynamic of the countertransference. In discussing imagery as a form of both resistance *and* communication, I draw on the research and writing of several psychoanalytic practitioners who discuss the often defensive processes that occur in the mainly hypnagogic state such as regression, resistance, avoidance, oscillation and visual gratification. These include Kris, Kanzer, Warren, Horowitz, Lewin, Ross and Kapp as well as material from contemporary clinical practice.

What I regard as the continuous and ubiquitous nature of the visual reverie or daydream is further developed in *Chapter 6 Visual reverie: the therapist's daydream* where I also look more closely at the responsive and collaborative nature of image construction that is occasionally manifest as an experience of shared or parallel imagery, with its clinical and interpretative implications. I draw again on the writings of American authors Isakower, Balter, Lothane and Spencer, Horowitz, Kern as well as on Bion's thoughts on reverie, in support of these ideas.

In *Chapter 7 Conclusion* I summarise my findings. I go over the steps by which I arrived at these, by drawing attention to the phenomenon of the apparent relegation of imagery within psychoanalytic discourse, the richness, complexity and significance of the therapist's daydream in relation to the patient, and the oscillating 'defensive-creative' role it plays within clinical practice. I have suggested that the therapist's ability to recognise and value the capacity for visualisation may not only enhance sensitivity to the patient's internal world thereby, providing a valuable tool for both theoretical understanding and analytic insight, but may also enrich the therapist's own experience of the work.

Notes

1 Freud first used the term 'psycho-analyse' in a French article (1896: 'L'hérédité et l'étiologie des néroses'. *S.E.*, 3:142–156) and in German in the same year (1896: 'Further Remarks on the Neuro-Psychoses of Defence' *S.E.*, 3:159–185; *G.W.* 1:379–403).

2   In these circumstances I make use in the first instance of a small technical device. I inform the patient that, a moment later, I shall apply pressure to his forehead, and I assure him that, all the time the pressure lasts, he will see before him a recollection in the form of a picture or will have it in his thoughts in the form of an idea occurring to him; and I pledge him to communicate this picture or idea to me, whatever it may be. He is not to keep it to himself because he may happen to think it is not what is wanted, not the right thing, or because it would be too disagreeable for him to say it. There is to be no criticism of it, no reticence, either for emotional reasons or because it is judged unimportant. Only in this manner can we find what we are in search of, but in this manner we shall find it infallibly. Having said this, I press for a few seconds on the forehead of the patient as he lies in front of me; I then leave go and ask quietly, as though there were no question of a disappointment: 'What did you see?' or 'What occurred to you?' This procedure has taught me much and has also invariably achieved its aim. Today I can no longer do without it.

3 In *Studies on Hysteria* (1893) Freud describes the process with Fräulein Elisabeth von R.: 'It was as though she were reading a lengthy book of pictures, whose pages were being turned before her eyes' (153).
4 For simplicity of writing, I designate the therapist as female and the patient as male, other than when using direct quotations or when the context specifically indicates otherwise.
5 By 'dimensional' I am referring generally to a sense of depth within the patient, and how this is perceived and addressed by the therapist. I discuss this in detail in Chapter 2, on 'spatiality'.

Chapter 1

What is a mental image?

… she decided in favour of seeing and began to describe her visual pictures.
(Freud 1893:277)

The question is simple and the response seems obvious, but to be clear, what I mean here by a mental image is some form of visual representation of an object, a scene, event, experience or idea that is held in the mind in the absence of any currently present physical manifestation. It may be clear and detailed, or vague and sketchy. Static, like a photograph, drawing or painting or moving like a video, a motion picture or something in between like a freeze-frame or slow motion form of action. Mental imagery may appear to the mind's eye in colour or monochrome, although black and white images would be linked to the age – and the aftermath of the age – of mechanical reproduction, as there would have been little experience of visualising in anything other than colour before the advent of either print or photography.

Mental images may appear in silence, or with some degree of accompanying sound, words, writing, bits of conversation, music or background noise. Some people report 'seeing' letters, words, numbers or sentences. In short, anything and everything that might appear in a dream can be regarded, in the waking state, as a mental image (although I am not here speaking of hallucinations). Further, the form of mental imagery with which I am at present concerned is not so much the images that may accompany immediate verbal or written descriptions, but more particularly the images that seem to appear at a tangent to, or somewhat removed from, any immediate stimulus through either direct or indirect associations. We can all imagine listening to someone describing an event to which we can relate by drawing on more or less shared experience. If a patient is describing, for example, a memory of trudging through snow to school aged six or seven, in the middle of December (something with which I am familiar) I will have no difficulty in visualising this generically, although the image in my mind may need to be altered or details adjusted to adapt to the particular narrative: a different era, geography, topography, language, architecture, accompanied or alone, safe or under bombardment and so forth. If a patient is describing trudging to school aged six or seven in the heat of a long tropical day, again in the middle of December, however, I have to draw on more than one kind of experience and somehow splice, overlay or merge together in my mind the familiar with the unfamiliar. Once again, this requires some adjusting, but is not too difficult to do, however distorted from reality the picture that emerges might be.

These are examples of mental imagery that comes about by simply picturing in one's mind something that is currently being described. If, on the other hand, a patient speaks of walking to school at the age of six or seven, in circumstances that are either familiar or alien to me and the picture that begins to emerge in my mind moves from the immediacy of the description as I find myself instead visualising the interior of a launderette somewhere in London, then my first thought upon noticing this would be: 'How did I get here?' I might feel that my attention had wandered. Perhaps it had, but maybe not – maybe the London launderette that emerged in my mind resonates with something my patient is telling me, however indirectly and however seemingly remote from the current narrative.

That is the sort of mental imagery I have in mind here, perhaps a form of 'visual' countertransference that, by dint of association, could be treated similarly to a conventional countertransference. Rather than hastily discarded as irrelevant, could it be something to be explored and questioned? Does this image belong to the therapist alone (thereby risking 'wild analysis'), or is there an unconscious association telling her something about the patient's emotional world that could be usefully understood through closer investigation of the thought behind the image, and therefore, worth keeping to one side of her mind as a note from the unconscious?

Drawing on experience

Soon after I began working as a psychotherapist, I started to notice this sort of apparently unrelated imagery appearing in my mind during a session. I would occasionally have an image in my mind's eye, whether vaguely or clearly that was seemingly unconnected to anything that was taking place in the session, or, if it was, then only indirectly. I paid scant attention to these images, since, while their occurrence was familiar, they seemed in themselves to be irrelevant. They did not often last beyond the session, and usually only for a fragment of the hour. They would rarely find their way into the notes that I would prepare either for myself, or for supervision, but something I simply regarded – if at all – as a kind of visual 'wallpaper'.

I could not have described them as intrusive, but when I did become aware of the picture in my mind, I would dismiss it as a distraction, and discipline myself to return to the more immediate content of the patient's communication. However, I gradually began to be more consciously aware of something like a pattern, in that a particular image or scene – usually of a place, or site, sometimes an event – would be frequently linked to a particular patient. On one occasion, mainly due to the awareness of an image that I began to recognise as

Figure 1.1 Sketch of mental image of corridor space.
Source: F. Carey.

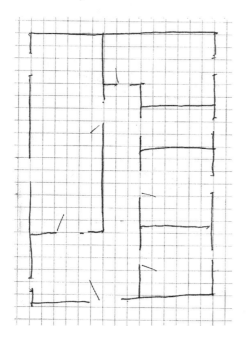

Figure 1.2 Sketch plan of corridor space.
Source: F. Carey.

persistent in relation to one particular patient, I included in my process notes a description of the imagery that had been in my mind, noting the detail as well as I could, alongside some of the associations that I linked to it. In writing it up, and then thinking about it, both on my own and during the following super-vision, it seemed to me that perhaps this apparently unrelated phenomenon had greater significance than I had hitherto thought, as the relevance to the patient became more significant.

I then began from time to time to note down these experiences and to think about their possible relevance, if any, to the patient during whose clinical hour they had occurred. When I could, I occasionally also made little sketches immediately after the session, if I could get hold of the image. Quite often, these took the form of plans of interior or exterior spaces, with sometimes a note of recognisable details.

In the session to which I briefly refer above, I had become aware that with this patient, a young woman, I would frequently have in my mind both the image of the interior of a flat, seen always from more or less the same position where the corridor ran through the space, a vantage point that enabled me to 'see' or imagine the whole of the interior. At the same time, I was also aware of the ground plan, one image somewhat superimposed on the other. As I was listening to the patient, the familiarity of the experience prompted me to imagine the plan of the space in my mind, and 'trace' it with my finger on my lap to help me remember it. After the session, I tried to sketch what I 'saw', which looked something like Figure 1.1.

I recognised the space as one with which I was somewhat familiar, but could not see the relevance of it with regard to the patient or the material. But I wrote it up and set it aside. I will come back to these later (Figures 1.1 and 1.2), in Chapter 6, 'Ms. A'.

Chapter 2

Spatiality, dimensionality and the visual

> Space may be the projection of the extension of the psychical apparatus.
> No other derivation is probable.
>
> (Freud 1938:300)

Space and dimensionality

A mental image needs a space in which to live. Of course, that 'space' is the mind, but not all minds seem to accommodate images equally. I have a colleague who seemed not to recognise this experience. When I asked her what came into her mind when I described, for example, walking to the supermarket, she replied that she saw in her mind's eye the word 'supermarket'. And when I asked her if she saw pictures in her dreams, she said that there may have – indeed, would have – been images there during the dream, but that her memory of the dream came to her as a verbal narrative. Personally, I can imagine seeing letters, words, sentences and numbers in the mind's eye, but I find it difficult to grasp not being able also to see images. Nevertheless, absence of imagery in processing ideas does not necessarily connote absence of dimensionality, but perhaps only a different style of processing ideas.

However, to think further about the place of mental imagery – in the context of psychotherapy – it is helpful to think first about the idea of *mental space,* the dimension within which the representation of objects is formed and held. I start from the understanding that the development of dimensionality, and a consequent sense of internal space, is essential for both emotional and intellectual growth, and that its absence can be understood as an indication of a disruption or impediment to that growth. Further, that the quality of this spatial dimension can often be both communicated and understood through processes that are themselves governed by dimensional development. This is so for the patient, and equally for the therapist, whose conscious and unconscious sensitivity to the nature of the patient's 'internal space' provides an effective therapeutic tool. In this chapter, I briefly review the role of spatiality in emotional development, and later go on to discuss modes of communication and perception of that dimension.

Spatiality and dimensionality in early psychoanalytic theory

Spatial themes are found within psychoanalytic theory and practice from very early on, but the subject begins to emerge more comprehensively around the mid-1960s with numerous references to aspects of spatiality and dimensionality, including descriptions that evoke ideas of space or place – either specifically or by inference – although it is not often the explicit subject of enquiry.

Quite early on, writing on *The Psycho-analysis of Space*, Paul Schilder (1935) remarks on both the subjectivity, and the essential split in the perception of space, noting that 'the space of the ego is preserved but that the space of the Id has undergone changes', and that, 'we live in a double orientation in space' (278). There is an objective space, but:

> We live our personal lives in relation to love objects, in our personal conflicts, and this is the space which is less systematized, in which the relations change, in which the emotions pull objects nearer and push them further away.... In this regressive space identifications and projections change the space and its value continually.
>
> (278)

In other words, we live simultaneously in both objective (measurable) and subjective (emotional or perceived) space.

'Fort-Da'

Although not intended as an essay on internal space, '*Beyond the Pleasure Principle*' (Freud 1920) contains a vignette that vividly expresses this idea (14–15). Freud's sensitive observation of his little grandson's repetitious 'fort/da' ('gone'/'there') game speaks of the child's creative management of his conflicted feelings at being separated from his mother. Grandfather watches the toddler who, with little language at his command, repeatedly dramatises what Freud comes to understand as the child's complex feelings around separation. Through action, gesture and vocalising, these uncomfortable experiences are projected outwards into both the actual as well as the symbolic world, expressing and to some extent, addressing the child's wish for mastery over its inner struggle with such feelings as loss, anxiety, helplessness, anger and aggression that he is not yet able otherwise to articulate. In doing so, we are also given a vivid illustration of internal space projected visibly, almost literally, into the external world.

In this domestic scene, Freud describes the child as normally 'well-behaved', with 'only a few words of vocabulary' and 'greatly attached' to his mother. Although he did not cry when she left him for short periods, Freud writes: 'This good little boy ... had an occasional disturbing habit of taking any small objects he could get hold of and throwing them away from him into a corner, under the bed, and so on' accompanied by 'a loud, long-drawn-out "o-o-o-o"', and 'an expression of interest and satisfaction' (14). Both his mother and grandfather agreed that this repeated sound had meaning, which they interpreted as 'fort' (German for 'gone'). Eventually, Freud realised as he watched the game unfold, that there was also, although not always, a sequel and that the child was not simply annoyingly throwing his toys away, but was rather inventing his own singular version of the universal game of hide and seek, providing himself with both the mystery and tension of 'lost', then the relief, joy and satisfaction of 'found'.

Freud was able to confirm his theory when one day he observed the child playing with a wooden reel with a piece of string attached that he would not pull along the floor as might be expected of a child of his age, but would instead:

> hold the reel by the string and very skilfully throw it over the edge of his curtained cot, so that it disappeared into it, at the same time uttering his expressive "o-o-o-o". He then pulled the reel out of the cot again by the string and hailed its reappearance with a joyful 'da' [German for "there"]. This, then, was the complete game—disappearance and return. As a rule one only witnessed its first act, which was repeated untiringly as a game in itself, though there is no doubt that the greater pleasure was attached to the second act.
>
> (14–15)

Freud notes that the little boy could only have regarded his mother's departure as disagreeable and through the invention of this game he finds a way to manage his inner conflict by repeating first, the distressing part of the experience – but as an event that he controls – then, subsequently, also gives himself the satisfaction of the second 'act', the 'joyful return' of the object, once again (by virtue of holding onto the string attached to the reel) entirely under his control. Freud notes, however, that while it was the first part of the game, making the object disappear, that was the most repeated element, it was the second part, the reappearance that gave him the greatest pleasure.

He concludes that the child benefited considerably from this exercise not only to gain mastery over frustration and helplessness by transforming distress into a game over which he has control, but also, as Freud states, 'to revenge himself on his mother for going away from him …', as if to say defiantly, 'All right, then, go away! I don't need you. I'm sending you away myself' (16) (although all the while keeping control of 'her', of course, by holding onto the string). This simple game exhibits quite sophisticated internal processes. It is an act of imagination and pretence, or 'play' that requires the ability to both hold an absent object in mind, then to endeavour to make meaning out of the confusing and painful experience within. Rather than suffer the helplessness of being abandoned the child transforms the feeling into one of complete control. At the same time, he is

Figure 2.1 'Fort-Da'.
Source: C. Carey.

demonstrating outwardly his developing capacity for symbolisation, representing his feelings through substitutive actions, gesture and sound. As can be seen, even at such an early stage, the symbol – here, a toy of the child's own invention – represents so much more than the sign.

In this well-known vignette, Freud depicts for us – in something that is very like a descriptive forerunner of Winnicott's formulation of transitional space – the baby's use of the space around him to manage his environment. The internal object is given external expression enabling the child to gain some control of, and possibly even triumph over, the disappearing object. This incidental observation provides us with a description of symbols, metaphors and gestures that give us a vivid picture of what may be going on within the child (rejecting and embracing internal objects), with only rudimentary sounds and expressions as additional clues to the many complex feelings concerning separation and reunion, and even the beginnings of such powerful feelings as revenge and forgiveness. So although absence generates anxiety, bearing absence (an element of the mourning process) enables the development of a sense of internal space where absent objects can be held imaginatively, and then symbolised through thought, play and gesture, as part of a growing personal internal landscape with a developing emotional and imagistic vocabulary, before language arrives and takes over.

The spatial dimension in developing psychoanalytic theory

This account was published in 1920, but the spatial metaphor within psychoanalysis is implicit, and perhaps unavoidable, even when not the specific subject of study. Right from the outset, in *Studies on Hysteria* (Breuer and Freud 1893) Freud's instinct is to employ a spatial allusion in describing the 'complicated and multi-dimensional organization' of pathogenic material as the 'defile' of consciousness that vividly captures numerous aspects of the substance of this enquiry. He states: 'Only a single memory at a time can enter ego-consciousness.' If the patient cannot relax his resistance:

> then the defile is, so to speak, blocked.... The whole spatially-extended mass of psychogenic material is in this way drawn through a narrow cleft and thus arrives in consciousness cut up, as it were, into pieces or strips. It is the psychotherapist's business to put these together once more into the organization which he presumes to have existed. Anyone who has a craving for further similes may think at this point of a Chinese puzzle....
>
> (291)

Freud's language is peppered throughout with ideas, words and phrases denoting mental geographies, embedded from early on in his conceptualisations of mental space. In several of his writings, he provides a sustained spatial metaphor of an agency guarding the entrance from one 'space' to another – that is, between unconscious, preconscious and conscious, in the first topography and, less concretely, between id-ego-superego, in the second.[1] He speaks of 'zones' 'anterooms' and 'frontiers' (Freud 1905); of censorship (Freud 1912b–1913), with its suggestion of divisions, borders and boundaries; the depiction of physically confined, but psychically unlimited dream-space (Freud 1900, 1923); the spatial reference implicit in the haunted spaces of the 'uncanny' (Freud 1919); and in the understanding of internal space as it develops through the processes of internalisation as described on p. 14 ('fort-da').

In *The Interpretation of Dreams* (Freud 1900), and elsewhere, Freud pursues the metaphor, stating: 'The crudest idea of these systems is the most convenient for us – a spatial one' (Freud 1915–1917:295ff.). He goes on to illustrate the concept through a sequence of rooms of different size and function within a building, whose thresholds are guarded by sentries vigilantly monitoring admission to these distinctive spaces, and where 'consciousness [is] a spectator at the end of the second room'. (Freud 1917:296)

In *The Uncanny* (Freud 1919), written at the same time as *Beyond the Pleasure Principle* (1920), a more layered idea of space emerges, rooted linguistically in the term itself, 'unheimlich', literally, 'un-homely', evoking the destabilising power of the idea, experience and meaning of 'home', wherein the most familiar of spaces is transformed into something frightening due to, Freud speculates, being 'traced back ... to something familiar that has been repressed' (247). Both of these contrasting ideas, the comforting (defensive) and the threatening (persecutory) internally held image, have a bearing on the discussion of visualisation which I come back to later (Chapter 5).

Memorably, too, in *Civilization and its Discontents* (Freud 1930), Freud again employs a spatial concept, in visually evoking the archaeology of Rome as an example of the indestructability of mental contents, however deeply buried or invisible. In the above examples, and many more, Freud's use of spatial imagery is striking, whether he is referring to actual events, or making use of a language that is full of visual descriptors: Rome and its many layers, the image of the gatekeeper or censor, the familiarity and the fear generated by the uncanny idea of 'home', the metaphorically geographic spaces of the mind, that not only create the context for meaning, but leave the reader with an indelible impression of these spaces peopled by figures, objects and events in space and time that make his intention clear, dimensional and memorable. The spatial aspect of his thinking and his theories, although not always explicit, is everywhere implied.[2]

Melanie Klein

Melanie Klein's approach was more specifically delineated, expressed as it was in terms of her principal hypothesis of projective identification implying or requiring a concept of an image (or imago)-laden, object-filled, three-dimensional space, however functional, dysfunctional or fragmented, necessary to accommodate the split-off and projected parts of the personality (Klein 1929:439).[3]

The theme is further extended in her description of 'positions' to portray the dynamic life of the internal object, with its emphasis on splitting and projection (Klein 1929, 1930, 1946), all metaphorically spatial terms. It was also more visceral, based on (primarily) hostile and persecutory infantile unconscious fantasies of the internal and external body of the mother – once again, all having spatial connotations. The link with the depressive position will be evident, underlining the correlation between the recognition and acceptance of loss, and the development of a sense of inner space, one that facilitates awareness of the difference between full (present) and empty (gone), an echo of 'fort-da'.

In her paper on symbol-formation (1930), Klein develops her ideas on inner space, a process again originating in the erotic and anxious fantasies pertaining to the body of the mother, and in particular in relation to the processes of movement between paranoid-schizoid and depressive positions. For such development to take place, an internal space must form.

Object Relations theory: Esther Bick's 'skin'

Building on Melanie Klein's construct of the nature of internal space, and based on pioneering work closely observing mother/infant interactions, Esther Bick's (1968) influential essay on the function of the skin in early object relations indicates that, in the primitive psyche, the skin functions as a boundary to hold the parts of the personality together until the infant is capable of introjecting an external object that it experiences as a reliable container, which if successful, enables a sense or fantasy of internal and external spaces. 'Until the containing functions have been introjected', she writes, 'the concept of a space within the self cannot arise'. Introjection, which Bick describes as 'the construction of an object in an internal space' cannot come about until there is an adequate internal space available (Bick 1968:484). Without this, the idea of projection or introjection is, by definition, premature.

Within the contemporary Kleinian tradition, Robert Hinshelwood (1997), in a paper detailing Esther Bick's contribution to understanding the role of the skin in relation to a sense of the integrity of the body, comments that 'the vicissitudes of internal space have become a crucial defining feature of Kleinian psychoanalysis' (308). He speaks of the skin creating:

> a sense of space, bounded space.... That space allows the processes and phantasies of passing objects in and out – projection and introjection. It also allows the experience of an object that has a space inside ... you cannot project into an object until you can have a conception of a space to project into. This is the defect in autism: no sense of a space inside the object.
>
> (309)

According to Bick, serious or prolonged disturbances in containment can give rise to a rigid, inflexible sense of self, sometimes seen as the development of a 'second skin'.

Winnicott's potential space

This 'second skin' idea also resonates with Donald Winnicott's (1965) notion of the development of the false self, one that emerges more in conformity with perceived external or environmental, rather than internal demands as a defensive or self-preservative measure.

But more pertinently with regard to this theme, Donald Winnicott's immensely influential writings (Winnicott 1953, 1967, 1968, 1971, 1974, 1986) could not be more explicit as expressions of the dimension of spatiality with regard to perceptual, intellectual and emotional development. His extensive work brings the language and concept of spatiality into common parlance with such terms as 'potential' and 'transitional' space to express the concept of movement and negotiation both within the self, and between subjects. In his idiosyncratic and at times paradoxical language, Winnicott defined 'potential space' as 'the hypothetical area that exists (but cannot exist) between the baby and the object ... at the end of being merged in with the object' (1971:107) describing a process of gradual, mutually negotiated separations. Here, what is needed for an idea to develop is an internal space where the absent object can be held. This space derives normally from the environment provided by the 'good enough' mother, first the womb, then her external body, then all the derivatives of holding that take place through growth, and significantly through play.

In her absence, what keeps the mother alive for the baby is the idea of the mother, and what is needed for an idea to develop, and be sustained, is an experience or sense that there is a space within, where this idea can be held. However, as separation is simultaneously necessary and threatening, the process is fraught with complexities and contradictions. If conditions are too menacing, then the risk is that defences develop against the opening up of such a space, inhibiting the capacity for imaginative play, or inner liveliness and collapsing the internal space essential for healthy separation and emotional growth. The experiences that give rise to such feelings mainly pre-date language, so that both current as well as later communications of this stage may take place through other means, via the body, gesture, enactment or imaging. In clinical terms, Winnicott suggests 'that psychotherapy is done in the overlap of two areas of playing, that of the patient and that of the therapist' (38). Winnicott's 'play space' provides Object Relations theory with a distinctly spatial platform – a metaphor that gains substance through the use and meaning of the space between subjects, and its overlap, whether that be the space of the therapeutic encounter, or any other interpersonal setting. Furthermore, precisely because this imagery is often prior to, or beyond words, it may risk being dropped from the language-privileged attention of clinical psychoanalysis, a theme I develop later.

However, the main theoretical references here are to those aspects of the work of Wilfred Bion (1956, 1962, 1970) and Donald Meltzer (1966, 1975a, 1975b, 1975c, 1992) that pertain to spatial development and dimensionality, emerging from both Freudian and Kleinian theories of the structure – or the construction – of the internal world.

Bion's containment

In a unique and distinctive effort to describe and refine processes of perception and communication in psychoanalytic understanding, Wilfred Bion evolved both a meta-theory and a system to enable what he regarded as a more objectively reliable hermeneutic understanding of degrees and levels of mental organisation. This development is schematised diagrammatically as a grid, an abstract representation of a progression of reflectivity that also provides the therapist with a mental map of the patient's internal world, the session and the process of therapy.[4] He writes, 'thoughts may be classified with the realizations of all objects approximating to the representation of three-dimensional space' (Bion 1970:11).

Bion's ideas of mental geometry and emotional mapping (1956), included concepts of such spatial categories as encapsulation, engulfment and concretisation. Of particular relevance to a psychoanalytic understanding of spatiality is his notion of a container and that which is contained within (Bion 1962). The mother's reverie, or her capacity to hold the infant in mind, provides the preeminent model of the relationship of objects, and of one's internal capacity for dimensionality that Bion regards as essential to the individual's ability to map the internal space necessary for thinking, linking and the making of meaning.

Continuing the spatial theme, Bion specifically refers to 'geometrical concepts of lines, points, and space' (emotional space as distinct from three-dimensional space) and suggests that the feeling of depression is 'the place where a breast or other lost object was' and that space is 'where depression or some other emotion used to be' (1970:10), that is to say there is a difference between spatial terms as used in common parlance, and those understood as mental images. He notes the distinction in complexity between the representation of 'multi-dimensional' geometric space, necessarily expressed two-dimensionally, and the 'multi-dimensional' space conceptualised by mental visual images, and goes on to postulate how such spatial considerations impact on the individual's capacity to map the internal space necessary for thought and the construction of meaning.

This distinction provides one of the areas of exploration here, in that in the clinical setting such intangible experience seeks a form of expression, which may elude language, exploiting instead silence, gesture, dream, daydream, reverie and other forms of expression, including enactments, alongside the patient's style and manner – all or any of which may be intuited through the therapist's conscious or unconscious imagery.

Bion's model of internal space is constructed on the foundation of Kleinian concepts of projective mechanisms, emphasising communicative aspects of the processes of splitting and projection, whereby projected feelings are modified by the mother's reverie (or its clinical equivalent) then returned 'detoxified' to the infant. This capacity is predicated upon a space of containment. Bion thus understood the internal world developing out of the infant's intimate physical relationship with its environment, with such experiences as the nipple in the mouth, or being held in the arms and mind of the mother, as prototypes of containment. He identifies this capacity as the mother's 'alpha-' function, and applies it to whatever subsequently stands in place of the mother's reverie. Failure of alpha-function 'involves the absence of mental visual images of points, lines and space' as if there are no geometric coordinates, and 'no conception of containers into which the projection could take place' adding 'the mental realization of space is therefore felt as an immensity so great that it cannot be represented ... at all' (Bion 1970:12). Such failure results in a formlessness, a persecutory, boundaryless, chaotic repository of 'bizarre objects', stuff, noise, unrelated disconnected, often menacing things, and the source of what he termed 'nameless dread' (Bion 1962:96). Clinically, what may 'appear to the observer as thoughts, visual images and verbalisations, are actually debris, remnants or scraps of imitated speech ... floating in a space so vast that its confines, temporal as well as spatial, are without definition' (Bion 1970:12–13).

Later, in Chapter 4, I go on to discuss how visualisation may operate as an expression of 'alpha-function' wherein the therapist sensually registers the character of the internal world of the patient through the clues of speech, language, figures of speech, speechlessness and other forms of both direct and indirect communication, providing an image – at greater or lesser levels of clarity and consciousness – that may be captured, processed and returned to the patient in a more meaningful form.

Meltzer's claustrum

While Bion's account of the inherent character of the internal world lies somewhere between Melanie Klein's often persecutory space based on the infant's fantasy of the body of the mother, and Winnicott's more benign inter-relational space, Donald Meltzer's research, influenced also by that of Esther Bick, explores these models further. In his paper on dimensionality (Meltzer 1975c), Meltzer suggests a programme for the normal development of psychic space, mapping the structure of a growing internal awareness of space and time, from one to four dimensions, based on increasingly sophisticated perceptions throughout early development. This space, or internal geography, incorporates the experience of inside and outside the self, as well as inside both internal and external objects. He stresses the link between growth in the perception of space, and the recognition and acceptance of the reality of time.

The earliest experiences of the self occupy a one-dimensional world where time and distance overlap and the relationship between self and object is undifferentiated – essentially a profoundly autistic world. Spatially, it is a description of a point, in which time and space are fused with little or no memory or sense of future. As the infant's experience of objects becomes associated with the sensual qualities of their surfaces, so the self is perceived as a sensual surface – a two-dimensional experience, highly sensitive, but limited. In this flat space, there is little capacity for experience to be held or contained. The space is in effect too shallow for sensation to be converted into thought or for thought to be encompassed and embodied. He posits and compares two types of identification, adhesive and projective, pointing out that where the two-dimensional world holds sway, the characteristic quality is lack of depth or shallowness, a paradoxically simultaneous denial of both intimacy and distance, which is at the same time a denial of absence, loss and time. Unable to tolerate separation, the individual wipes it out by flattening or discrediting, the space in which separation could come about or separateness could exist, and therefore, also, the space of the absent object that could nonetheless be held in the mind. Clinically, this may manifest itself in numerous ways that can be understood as dimensional. Such individuals may experience a form of emotional or relational paralysis, lack of affect, premature and defensive intellectualisation – phenomena that have a bearing on my argument with regard to verbalisation and visualisation.

With time, and a growing tolerance for delay, the infant encounters a resistance to penetration in the object that conveys an awareness of shape – a solid, boundaried form beyond the perceived limits of its own body. This gives rise to a sense of entering or moving into and around a depth or a solid, rather than merely piercing a simple surface. The object – and by extension, the self – is now felt to have substance, depth and dimensionality, both embodying, containing and occupying space. Meltzer observes that this capacity is directly related to an effective sphincter-function and the establishment of a sense of a secure container – a place or a mind in which one can hold, and be held, as opposed to a surface to which one clings.

The experience of movement from inside to outside an object coincides with a perception of time, the idea of 'before', 'now', 'then' corresponding to something like the experience of front, middle, back and a consequent sense of both form and continuity. Here, both boundaries and the early intimations of separateness, have their roots. The individual now has a sense of containment, a space within which it can retain the idea of the object over a period of time and begins to inhabit a four-dimensional world of both time and space where objects are gradually recognised as being outside one's omnipotent control. In further exploring the nature of internal space (Meltzer and Williams 1988), the authors note that beyond the distinction 'between the public and private spaces of the individual' they also consider the distinction between 'private', or that which recognises an external audience, and 'secret', indicating that which is protectively inward. These experiences find expression in the distinction 'between internal and external worlds in our model of the mind' (79).

Meltzer argues that disruptions in thinking and linking, as described by Bion (1959a), are further characteristics of a state of mind, where a space in which ideas may be held and processed, is annihilated. In the clinical setting, such manifestations of both verbal and non-verbal behaviour may be understood as, inter alia, expressions of the nature of the dimensionality of the patient's internal world that, as I suggest later, may be inferred through the analyst's internal and spatial imagery. He suggests that the consequences of the failure of this process is a life lived more 'in the claustrum' than in the world, showing up in characteristics such as shallowness, or 'empty-headedness', and in such behaviours as clinging, tactile or visual attachment to stimulating surfaces, copying or other forms of accommodation, as manifest, for example, in Winnicott's false self (1971), in which compliance with external rather, than internal, demands dominates.

Clinical example: Mr. B

Something of this feature of limited dimensionality or impenetrability may be illustrated in work with a patient whose lack of dimensional development extended to something bordering on a dread of the experience of an internal space within which objects can be held.

Mr. B was a young man whose own training as a health care professional required that he do a certain amount of psychoanalytic reading. He found the idea of Winnicott's 'potential space' not so much difficult to understand, as terrifying, almost repulsive, to think about. It made him shudder. In the early days of treatment, he would come hesitantly into the room, slope-shouldered, and occupy as little space as possible. Often throughout the session, he would nestle into the corner of the couch with arms wrapped round drawn-up knees. When speaking, his voice was unexpressive except for a tendency to end statements as if with a question mark. He had a habit of not completing sentences, but would speak rather in phrases that were thematically connected, but broken, such as 'Yesterday, I saw Mary(?) ... it's been years(?) ... this is someone who ... it reminded me that ... I didn't want ... I wonder if she saw me?' When he did say something that could be construed more as a complete statement, he very soon felt compelled to retract or modify it. If I responded, he would almost invariably do the same with my sentence: cut it up, modify it, tinker with it – like playing with food without eating it (which is what his mother describes him as having done as a toddler and which he claims still to do), as if nothing would be allowed past his mouth into something that could be experienced as a gut, where it could be processed.

Mr. B was very thin and, although in his late 20s, his physical development seemed to be arrested almost at the stage of adolescence. It transpired that he had little sense of internal organs, especially anything that could be construed as a container within himself, such as lungs, stomach, and bowel nor was there much sense of a space that could accommodate them. He felt his inside to be tubular and solid, and graphically described it as being like a stick of rock, made up of something undifferentiated and homogenous inside with little or no capacity to retain anything of substance within. However, he did dream quite vividly, although sometimes the dreams were difficult to describe in words, as they were more like sensations. One dream, quite nightmarish and recurring from late childhood or early adolescence, was of a taut length of cable or wire stretched along a shallow ditch upon which he was obliged to move as if transported, a form of endless extension of his own self, accompanied by a whine that, when it reached a certain pitch would spell his annihilation.

Alongside the fragmenting of his sentences, over time it became noticeable that his speech, whether of current incidents, memories, thoughts, dreams or general descriptions, contained repeated images that had in common the characteristics of flatness and impenetrability. These included the images described above: cable; wire; rope; rock; as well as stoppers; corks; cardboard; paper; glue; damaged surfaces such as things being torn, ripped, scratched, bitten (not quite penetrating); and numerous descriptions of things happening on thresholds. This accumulation of images began to form something like a gallery, or exhibition of imagery in which we could detect a theme that had to do with a fear or a repulsion at the idea of having an inside, a personal internal space, in which feelings and experiences – especially those that were aggressive or damaging – could be held. The idea of such a space felt threatening to him, as did Winnicott's 'potential space', and represented something menacing and abhorrent, resembling Bion's 'nameless dread'. It was a mystery to him how such an idea could ever be conceived of as something welcome or creative.

Space exploration: further developments of spatiality in psychoanalytic theory

Marion Milner (1952) explores spatiality through her patient's symbolic[5] use of the objects and spaces of the consulting room. Later (1969), she describes work that communicates the subjective experience of internal and external space, defining an interior landscape that originates in the containing space of the womb and provides 'the inner awareness of one's own body [through] a slow creating of a concept of an inner containing space...' (122). She sees the construction of inner space as fundamentally somatic, deriving from such primitive experiences as the rhythm of the mother's heart and breath as indicators of shape and pace; her holding of the infant and the experience of the nipple in the mouth, providing a sense of a body with an outside and an inside, a mouth that can be explored with one's own tongue – and so sense a personal inner space that is enriched and extended by the shift from oral to anal libidinal zones, through the experience of a gut and a rectum. She understands that such an exploration enables a construction of one's 'inner containing space' that can be investigated through the experience of the body, 'by directing attention inwards'. She revisits the concept of libidinal zones and the transference of conflict 'from the inner space of the mouth to the inner space of the rectum' (Milner 1969:124). She speaks also of the creation of 'one's own inner frame ... in which one holds a kind of inner space' and 'one of the earliest roots of such a capacity might be the experience of being held in one's mother's arms...' (250). Milner indicates five components necessary for the construction of such inner space: mouth, tongue and nipple; hands; rectum; mother's arms; and the ability to separate from the mother, a formulation later expanded upon by Harold Stewart (1985) to include the vagina and the womb – two components physically absent from the male experience of personal inner space, but perhaps present psychologically and experienced as a void.

Others, including Roger Money-Kyrle (1968), James Grotstein (1978) and Christopher Bollas (1982) have since both critiqued and expanded upon these theories, providing further observations concerning the ability to take in and retain, the capacity for closeness and distance within relationships, the development of self-reflection, as well as the use and range of language that indicates spatial and dimensional development, or the lack of it as may be manifest in feelings such as claustrophobia, agoraphobia, acrophobia, flatness and so forth. Others, such as Bassin (1982), draw attention to the experience of inner space as gendered, with physiological distinctions providing a core determinant in the formation of body ego and self-representation.

Turning to a body of thought generated by Winnicott's (1953, 1971) theories of the relationship between fantasy, reality and imaginative thought, as expressed through the concepts of transitional space and potential space, Thomas Ogden (1985) extended these ideas in relation to both play space and analytic space. He details the development of a spatial dimensionality from mother-infant unity, through to the 'capacity to be alone in the presence of the mother' (185) and describes the characteristics of the corresponding transference and countertransference experiences, bringing together key themes that I wish to consider further here. He sees the failure to engage with potential space as a failure of psychological dialectics, with a consequent collapse of symbolisation. Later, Ogden (1989) explores a specific area of primitive experience that he has defined elsewhere (1988) as 'autistic-contiguous', extending Bick's (1968), Meltzer's (1975a, 1975b), and Francis Tustin's (1980, 1984) theories based on Bion's (1962) Winnicott's (1971) and Fairbairn's (1944) Object Relations theories. This state refers to an internal oscillation between isolation and connectedness, and a manner of constructing meaning and identification from sensory impressions, generating 'the sense of a bounded sensory surface' (Ogden 1989:129), within which a developing awareness of self is located.

A number of writers have observed the manifestation of internal space as it translates into analytic space – an aspect of the area of study with which I am particularly concerned – an example being Serge Viderman (1974) who speaks of the co-construction of an analytic space, which is both physical, consisting of 'a space confined by four walls, objects of the material world which have shape and weight, a couch and an armchair' (470), but also, imaginary, a discrete space where the analytic process can develop, including enabling the patient's free association and, its corollary, the analyst's freely-floating attention. In this space, however, where shared consciousness develops through reverie and speech, Viderman addresses a number of distortions, which arise as a result of the opacity and ambiguities of language, giving clinical examples that emphasise the image or spatial image, as precursor to thought and language. Using Freud's case study of 'Dora' (Freud 1905) to illustrate his thesis, Viderman says:

> This difference between analytic situation and analytic space is so evident in the analysis of Dora that it enables us to perceive more clearly the nature of the one and the other, to justify the concept of space and to single out its contribution to a theory of analytic technique.
>
> (477)

These several perspectives on spatiality – actual, metaphorical, projective, linguistic and clinical – I hope will help to locate the substance of my argument within a spatial context and function with regard to the capacity for the development and use of imagery, for both patient and therapist.

Summary

Here, I am mainly concerned with how understanding the development and function of spatiality and dimensionality contribute towards a capacity for visualisation in both patient and therapist and, further, how this capacity also enables the therapist to better comprehend the patient's internal world through a counter-transference response to the patient's communication of his or her dimensional development. This experience may be provoked by language, figures of speech, speechlessness, voice, tone and numerous forms of both silence and non-verbal communication, gesture, mood, manner, style and other means of communication, as processed through the therapist's own, often unconscious, often unacknowledged, capacity for representation.

Notes

1 The idea of agencies guarding these boundaries first appears in a letter to Fleiss of 22 December 1897 (Masson 1985:289) where Freud indicates that a form of censorship is activated that endeavours to make meaning unintelligible, identified by Laplanche and Pontalis as 'placed at the point of original repression' (1973:66).

2 Donald Meltzer (1968) disagrees, stating that Freud did not conceptualise spatially, due to his neurophysiological preconceptions and the hydrostatic model of instinct, stating: 'Nowhere in his writings is there a conceptualization of spaces' other than, to some extent, in the Schreber case, where he talks about the world destruction fantasy.'

3 In this same essay (440), Klein develops ideas on internal space with an account of a woman whose despair is experienced as an unfillable empty space within that Klein associates to the evocation of both the empty or absent breast, as well as to the (girl's) fear of retaliation for the fantasied attack on the mother's body.

4 Bion first presented the 'Grid' in 1963, to the British Psycho-Analytic Society.

5 Symbol-formation, a central concept in Klein's (1930) developmental theory and the subject of a seminal paper by Ernest Jones (1916), was addressed by Marion Milner (1952) who emphasises its more progressive, developmental aspects – finding the familiar in the unfamiliar – as opposed to the more defensive or regressive function, as characterised by both Klein and Jones.

Chapter 3

Unconscious communication

Projection, projective identification, reverie and countertransference

> It is a very remarkable thing that the Ucs. of one human being can react upon that of another, without passing through the Cs. This deserves closer investigation but, descriptively speaking the fact is incontestable.
>
> (Freud 1915:194)

Projective processes

In this section, I review ideas about projective processes, focusing on the countertransference experience, through the lens of the visual element in the session, by considering a range of perspectives offered by various thinkers on the subject over time.

Freud first spoke of the concept of 'projection' in 1895 in his correspondence with Wilhelm Fleiss describing it as a defence against intolerable feelings that are dealt with by expelling them outside oneself and attributing such feelings to a specific other, or others. The idea was developed by followers, such as Karl Abraham and Freud's daughter Anna, but most emphatically by Melanie Klein (1946), who stressed its place in infant development particularly with regard to the central dynamic of splitting, and in the context of the ambivalent connection to the mother as the generic model upon which later relationships are based. As a consequence, anxious fantasies ensue concerning the fate of both the depleted and damaging self as well as the manipulated and damaged object. Klein significantly expanded the concept to include the idea of projective identification, in which split-off parts of the self are forced into others and are lodged there, engendering a fragmented or scattered sense of self (102). Klein initially understood, or at least described this process in pathological terms, but eventually regarded it as also developmental, a primitive process of the infant psyche that would become modified over time. These unconscious processes are implicitly spatial, since – as discussed previously – it requires some sense, however primitive or embryonic, of inside and outside the self, of an object beyond and a boundary between self and object. In the 70 or more years since Klein's seminal work on the subject, the immense discourse surrounding the concept has both broadened and deepened its meaning, and its usage has been significantly modified.

However, although projection and projective identification may be – and have been – intricately described and fulsomely illustrated clinically, precisely how these processes actually take place remains a matter for conjecture and specula-tion, other than to say that – descriptively speaking – it is rooted in the primitive psyche, is often marked by a sense of urgency or anxiety, and may have an unex-pected and forceful impact on the intended object (both within and beyond the clinical setting).

Hanna Segal (1974) succinctly defines projective identification, stating, 'parts of the self and internal objects are split-off and projected into the external object, which then becomes possessed by, controlled and identified with the projected parts' (14). She expands upon the concept to include 'primitive projective reparation' (27–28) to incorporate both loving and hateful feelings. Further, both clinical experience and everyday life also attest to the disturbing power of such mechanisms, whether aggressive or libidinal and, in the clinical setting, their capacity to disrupt the analyst's ability to process the patient's communications is widely noted. This disruption may provoke modes of enactment, but may also take other more subtle forms, such as daydreaming, wandering attention, listless-ness or the formation of spontaneous imagery, all of which are discussed more fully later. At such times, processing the material through imaging may become more prominent, either defensively, if the thought is disturbing or complex, or as a substitute, however temporary, for more formal conceptualisation. While the disruptive power of projection has been well reported, its contribution to enhanc-ing insight into the patient – equally well-documented – is unmistakable, and at the heart of analytic understanding, unconscious to unconscious.

Clinical impact of projective processes

Thomas Ogden (1979), in discussing the role of projective identification in the countertransference, agrees with Winnicott's definition of the 'objective counter-transference' (1949:70) as basically the complement to the patient's transference whereby 'the therapist allows himself to participate to an extent in an object rela-tionship that the patient has constructed on the basis of an earlier relationship' (Ogden 1979:370), thus, enabling an understanding of the patient's emotional experience derived from the therapist's capacity for identification. Ogden regards a defensive reluctance, or inability, on the part of the therapist to participate in this somewhat risky process as detrimental to the therapy, not only in terms of the lost opportunity of the emotional encounter in a fresh setting, but more insid-iously, in the therapist's unwittingly taking up the role assigned him by the patient as a form of unconscious enactment.

This echoes Bion's (1959) description of the infant's compulsion to forcefully project into an object that seems otherwise impenetrable to its needs, which may then be repeated or re-enacted in the clinical setting. Bion emphasises the element of manipulation as a characteristic feature of the identificatory com-ponent of the mechanism, such that the analyst, as container or recipient of the projection, feels somehow coerced into 'playing a part … in somebody else's phantasy' (Bion 1961:49). Once again, from the standpoint of the object, it is not clear how the projection comes to be taken up, or how this coercive dynamic comes about other than to note that these processes are for the most part both unconscious, involuntary and passive.

This idea is consistent with an aspect of visualisation that I discuss later (see Chapters 5 and 6) concerning the therapist's experience of 'discovering' herself somewhere in her imagination, but uncertain as to how she got there: the site, situation or setting may not appear to relate immediately to this patient, or to what the patient is speaking of specifically, yet may nonetheless, seem to have a consistency or perseverance in relation to a particular patient, such that when projective processes are more active or vivid, the site, space, place or context of the visualisation comes to be a recognisable component of that patient's 'setting' in the mind of the therapist. In spite of its persistence, however, this perception may take some time to register and its consistency may be recognised only retrospectively.

Ogden (1979:363) describes these primitive communications as 'quasi-telepathic' (borrowing the term from Spitz, 1965) and visceral in character (see also Grinberg 1962). Harold Searles (1963) speaks of the therapist's openness to the patient's projections as a necessary 'participation in the patient's "delusional transference"' (275), not to be confused with countertransference psychosis. While this may be true, insofar as it suggests a willingness to engage with the more disturbed aspects of the patient, nonetheless, it remains unclear as to how this counsel is to be followed in the way Searles suggests – given that all aspects of the process are unconscious – other than to be aware of, familiar and in touch with one's own defensive tendencies.

Finding the balance between emotional participation and self-containment is a matter of clinical poise, particularly as the patient exerts pressure upon the therapist to conform to the projective fantasy. When this happens, such fantasies may manifest in the form of images, sometimes very fleeting, yet nonetheless, offering a glimpse of a distinctive significance specific to this particular patient, or this patient-therapist dyad. Many therapists will recognise that being perceived differently by different patients, sometimes radically so, has an impact on the therapist's self-perception during the session in the sense of actually feeling, and at times even sounding and behaving, for example, more like either an idealised – or demonised – parent, boss, teacher, spouse, partner, sibling and so forth, yet all the while having to stay in touch with one's own sense of self. However, these transient and oscillating self-states – forms of temporary mini-enactments – serve to inform the therapist of the patient's relationship to his objects, and such perceptions may often arise through or be enhanced by, one's own store of imagery and imagistic self-perception.

Herbert Rosenfeld (1987) touches on the phenomenon of the impact of the patient's projective identification on the analyst when he describes forms of such excessive identification that 'there is a danger that the verbal communication between patient and analyst may break down' and the 'patient's communications increasingly assume a concrete quality' (161–162). This then interferes with the capacity for abstract thinking in the therapist, blurring the boundary between reality and fantasy, and making it difficult for the analyst to make, and the patient to make use of, verbal interpretations. It is then important to try to discern the projective processes that are being employed. Here I suggest (and describe more fully in Chapters 5 and 6) that a product of such projective processes may come in the form of imagery that arises spontaneously in the mind of the therapist, and may prove an effective tool in both accelerating and deciphering this process, providing a route through an impasse where the force of the projections may inhibit or prevent verbal articulation, yet leave imagery not only untouched, but possibly even more vivid.

Michael Feldman (1997) considers the analyst's involvement in the patient's projective processes, and notes that since Heimann's (1950) and Racker's (1958) seminal papers on countertransference (see pp. 37–38 further on in this chapter), emphasis has increasingly been placed on observing 'the way in which the patient's phantasies … may come to influence the analyst's state of mind and behaviour' especially 'as a source of information concerning the patient's unconscious mental life—his internal object relations in particular' (Feldman 1997:228). His view is that the patient uses projective identification to coerce the therapist into living out some aspect of the patient's internal object relations and cites David Tuckett's (1995, at the time unpublished) research on mutual enactment, stating: 'Enactment makes it possible to know in representable and communicable ways about deep unconscious identifications and primitive levels of functioning which could otherwise only be guessed at or discussed at the intellectual level' (ibid.).

I suggest that visual fantasy, while not normally an enactment, may be regarded as a site on the continuum of such processes. Becoming aware of background or foreground imagery or developing an awareness of a spatial component in the analyst's spontaneous associations, can be a means of discovering responses that may otherwise be inaccessible to her conscious attention, not only, but including, those situations where the material may be of a complex or disturbing nature.

Further, the spontaneous image, under certain conditions, may be more effective at evading the critical scrutiny of internal censorship than the precision of thought formulated through language, and habituating oneself to awareness of such imagery is a step towards identifying its therapeutic potential. However, and paradoxically, under other conditions, mental imagery may be itself a source of anxiety, which *arouses*, rather than evades internal censorship: this contradictory and oscillating function of imagery is a core theme here, and I discuss these competing dynamics more fully later (see Chapters 5 and 6).

The visual countertransference

In considering the projective phenomenon of countertransference, I am focusing primarily on its visual and spatial aspects that I regard as potentially shedding light on the internal world of the patient through attending to those responses that come to the attention of the analyst in the form of imagery. In that specific regard, it will be useful to review some ideas on countertransference to establish a context for this approach.

Attitudes to countertransference experience have undergone radical shifts since 1910, when Freud identified the counterpart to the patient's transference as that which 'arises in him as a result of the patient's influence on his unconscious feelings' (1910a:144), although the exact meaning of this term was, and remains, both imprecise and controversial. Freud originally warned of the danger to objectivity presented by the phenomenon, an attitude that remained largely in place until Paula Heimann's (1950) decisive revisiting of the concept, and the continuing discussion that has ensued, with countertransference now regarded by almost all psychoanalytic practitioners as a key tool in both heuristic and interpretative processes crafted primarily by the Kleinian development of the concept of projective identification, as summarised broadly and very briefly, above.

With this development there came an essential shift in the position of the therapist in relation to the patient. Recognition of the dynamic place of the countertransference within the therapeutic process acted for some as a form of 'equaliser', allowing the therapist access to ideas, practices and creative processes that previously seemed professionally, and occasionally ethically, inaccessible, enfolded as they were within the psychoanalytic stance defined as 'abstinence'.

In his paper on countertransference communication, Christopher Bollas (1983) indicates that through verbal, non-verbal and pre-verbal self-states, patients create unique environments that generate numerous, nuanced mental states in the analyst that include 'passing images, and fantasies' (2) that the analyst then endeavours to process and reflect back to the patient. Bollas describes these countertransference responses often in spatial terms, and advocates the use of such responses to place important material into a mutually useable space, with particular emphasis on the insight gained concerning the patient's relationship to his objects.

This reading of countertransference as a spatial construct is reinforced by Norbert Freedman (1997), who states:

> For an analyst to sustain an optimal state of listening, he or she will create a house, a container, that holds within it dimensions of listening space. When the analyst hears the story, visualizes the scenario, senses the affect, dreams along with the patient ... this is the space of empathic attunement.
>
> (83)

So, paying attention to and developing, this capacity to experience the patient's material in spatial and visual terms may enable a dimensionally richer understanding of the internal world, particularly where the therapist's defensive responses are aroused, for whatever reason. This approach requires recognition of, and at times confrontation with, a number of obstacles – some of which are relevant to this enquiry, particularly insofar as they touch upon the internal fantasy of the therapist, and the use to which it is put.

Visual and spatial aspects of the countertransference: development of theories and practices

In the following overview of some aspects of the development of the concept and clinical application of countertransference I am concerned mainly with its relationship to, and impact upon, the therapists' experience of visual imagery, whether their patients' or their own. In his works intended for publication, Freud appears to have mentioned the 'counter-transference' only twice, first when he writes:

> We have become aware of the "counter-transference", which arises ... as a result of the patient's influence on [the analyst's] unconscious feelings, and we are almost inclined to insist that he shall recognize this counter-transference in himself *and overcome it* [my emphasis].
>
> (Freud 1910a:145–145)

The second appearance of the term arises five years later (1915) when he states: 'In my opinion, therefore, we ought not to give up the neutrality towards the patient, which we have acquired through keeping the counter-transference in check' (164). The term also appears in letters to both Jung and Binswanger, from around the same time (Freud 1910b, 1911, 1913b, 1915).

Although these may have been the earliest public outings of the term, the fact of countertransference[1] – a concept whose meaning and value have shifted radically in the intervening years from something to be defensively 'overcome' to something prized as a clinical touchstone – was in evidence from the very outset, at the centre of the relationship between Breuer and Anna O., in the neonatal phases of psychoanalysis.

In these early statements, Freud introduces both the concept of countertransference – and he appears to have been speaking exclusively of the erotic countertransference – and the ambiguities inherent within it. The uncertainty regarding its source or site, whether it is lodged solely in the unconscious of the analyst, is the projection of the patient, or is somehow constructed jointly, is already intimated here. Whatever the uncertainties, from the time of the earliest days of the 'scientific project', Freud had sensed both the 'opportunities' and 'threats' it might pose to the young science. The defensiveness surrounding the phenomena is explicit in the letter to Jung where he writes '... I believe an article on "counter-transference" is sorely needed; of course we could not publish it, we should have to circulate copies among ourselves' (Freud 1911).

Although Freud is clear that 'enactment' within the analytic setting is an impediment and the analyst must not succumb to the seduction of (returning) the patient's love, the ambiguity with regard to countertransference as implement or impediment is there from the start (Freud 1910a, 1915). Between these two papers, Freud introduced the idea of 'empathic attunement', suggesting the analyst 'must turn his own unconscious like a receptive organ towards the transmitting unconscious of the patient...' However, to be able to use his unconscious as a receptive instrument in analysis, the analyst 'may not tolerate any resistances in himself which hold back from his consciousness what has been perceived by his unconscious' (Freud 1912:115–116). It is this understanding of the term, the analyst's use of her unconscious as a receptive instrument – in this case one that responds also through imagery, or what I call the 'visual countertransference' – that is the principle use of the term here.

Shifting attitudes

In the ensuing years, although there was much written on the analyst's attitude – that of detachment, empathy, the therapeutic alliance, the impact of transference and so forth – countertransference was mentioned, but rarely as a subject of discrete enquiry. And while the lengthy and extensive debate concerning the source, legitimacy and value of the countertransference has, over the years, enriched both the discourse and the practice of psychoanalysis, being as infused as it was with such deep-rooted anxiety and defensiveness, has meant that both the analytic and interpretative potential for countertransference experience took time to gain legitimacy, respectability and currency. It was initially deemed unworthy of serious discussion other than precautionary, and seen often as an indication of the analyst's inadequacies, imperfections and consequent need for further analysis. Indeed, Cole (1922), for one, includes it as the 10th of her 20 recommendations of 'Don'ts' for beginners practising 'psycho-analysis': 'Don't fail to note signs of a counter transference. These will be found in the analyst's dreams and should be dealt with immediately. A counter transference means the need for further analysis for the analyst' (44). However, an opposing school of thought was developing as early as 1927 with such individual thinkers as Sandor Ferenczi who recommended acknowledging feelings for and about the patient and, furthermore, expressing them as part of the treatment, a view with which only a minority concurred.

Numerous early writers (Glover 1927a, 1927b; Reich 1933; Fenichel 1938) also noted the relationship between countertransference and resistance to aspects of the patient, or his material, with the risk that the analyst may suppress his or her instinctive reactions to the patient, a consequence detrimental to treatment, since it would be a form of emotional withdrawal equivalent to resistance in the patient. This theme of resistance to the impact of the patient is a persistent one within the discourse on the subject, and is significant here, in terms of both forming, recognising, as well as avoiding responsiveness through imagery.

It was not until the 1950s that the phenomenon, through both private discussion and open debate, had gradually accrued sufficient serious attention – following pioneering work by those mentioned above as well as Bálint and Bálint (1939), Sharpe (1947) and Winnicott (1949) – to enable a less defensive, more imaginatively critical approach. In 1957, Michael Balint wrote: 'The interrelation of the transference of the patient and the counter-transference of his analyst is in the focus of attention right from the start, and remains there' (299). Over time, fantasies of perfection and idealisation of the process, which the profession as a whole has found – and often continues to find – difficult to relinquish, have gradually yielded to the more realistic and indeed more creative recognition that the countertransference is not only an unavoidable, but an essential response, one to be welcomed in the pursuit of working both intuitively as well as professionally. Shared clinical experience over time afforded recognition of the value of judicious use of the countertransference, and encouraged a more relaxed as well as a more dynamic approach to its place in clinical practice, particularly through greater confidence in the mechanism of free association, for both patient and therapist.

The shift towards recognition of the value of the countertransference was gradual and turned on a re-evaluation of the role, and the actual, rather than idealised, experience of the therapist in the clinical setting. Between 1949 and 1957 a spate of influential papers was published, which established the broad parameters of countertransference within both theory and practice, beginning with Winnicott's (1949) short, radical and ultimately liberating essay that identified and legitimised, the analyst's 'hate' in the countertransference – primarily, but not exclusively, in work with psychotic patients. He did not consider this response the product of inadequate analysis, but one that is akin to the natural – although, at the time, largely unacknowledged or unadmitted – hatred a mother feels for her infant, but overcomes through overriding love and concern, parallel to the work that the analyst must do professionally with regard to the patient (70).

Winnicott also advocated a form of disclosure of this process in due course, usually towards the end of treatment, suggesting that an analysis is incomplete if at some point the analyst is unable to share something of this experience with the patient (74). Writing in the same year, Berman (1949) concurs with this viewpoint, and understands the patient's intuitive witnessing of the analyst's struggle with loving and hateful feelings within the countertransference as evidence of the process through which realistic and well-integrated functioning is achieved and is, as such, a transformative factor in the therapy, similar to the description of the infant's experience of the mother's 'reverie' (see Chapter 6). Issues concerning both recognition, as well as disclosure, of negative feelings have implications for aspects of my thinking, notably with regard to forms of internal 'scotomisation', denial of thoughts and associations, and other defensive strategies concerning the visual form of countertransference that I discuss later (Chapter 5).

A major contribution to this shift in attitude was Paula Heimann's concise essay, *On Counter-transference* (1950) that marked this divergent trend indelibly. Although the tide was beginning to turn, her paper (which, according to Sandler, was 'the first explicit statement of the positive value of the counter-transference' [1976:43]) was nonetheless written against the grain of the still prevailing attitude within analytic circles, that the countertransference was nothing but trouble.

Heimann added something new in maintaining that the analyst's unconscious understands that of the patient's and the countertransference covers all feelings that the analyst experiences towards the patient, not only those attributable to transference. She recognised the transference as the 'instrument of research into the patient's unconscious', but the analyst must also be able to recognise and consult his or her own feelings, in the service of deeper understanding and interpretation. This skill is embodied in the technique, central to analytic practice, of 'evenly hovering' or 'freely-floating' attention – the counterpart to the patient's free associations – enabling the analyst to listen 'simultaneously on many levels' (1950:81–82) on the one hand, and on the other, to be aware of his own free ranging responses, including registering his own emotional reactions to the patient and his story. Here, I add that these free ranging responses would include those that come in visual form.

Margaret Little's (1951) contribution was somewhat more cautious, suggesting the countertransference may arise out of a primitive, paranoid, persecutory anxiety, altering analytic activity from a heuristic to a defensive process in which both analyst and patient are collusively protecting each other, with the analyst shifting from the more beneficial introjective to the more defensive projective identification with the patient (35). Little's chief concern regarding misuse of the countertransference is where it derives from unanalysed, repressed elements within the analyst, that correlate to the patient's transference. This understanding of countertransference as (also) a paranoid, defensive position has a bearing on the discussion (Chapters 4 and 5) concerning both the construction and the dynamic use of imagery in the clinical setting, in which I suggest that countertransference anxieties may evoke imagery as a form of refuge or retreat.

Annie Reich (1951), who reserves the term for the effects of the analyst's unconscious internal conflicts, comments upon the spontaneous nature of insight into the patient's material that occasionally comes about effortlessly, and not as a result of any active thinking on the part of the analyst, as if through a sudden, temporary, but intense identification with the patient. The phenomenon, which may be provoked by either the patient or the analytic situation, provides a tool for understanding that derives from the analyst's own unconscious, facilitated by a capacity to listen with 'freely-floating attention'. Once again, this observation may apply also to the spontaneous imagery that emerges effortlessly into the mind of the analyst, potentially shedding light on the patient's internal situation. I would describe this as an aspect of visual countertransference phenomena, that may certainly, but not exclusively, be rooted in the unconscious of the analyst, deriving from past or present personal internal conflicts, but that may nonetheless, reflect a similar dynamic within the patient. Elements of this understanding are illustrated in the examples later in this chapter.

Working at much the same time, but independently and in Argentina, Heinrich Racker was developing his ideas on the phenomenon and value of the countertransference, and took the enquiry substantially further than his contemporaries in Europe. His first highly influential paper on the subject (1953)[2] touches on Winnicott's theme of 'hate in the countertransference' (Winnicott 1949), published four years later, but written at about the same time. Racker suggests that – echoing the process within the patient – the analyst's images, feelings and impulses towards the patient, insofar as they are determined by his past, may be considered as the 'countertransference' proper, and their pathological expression as the 'countertransference neurosis'. Here, if the analyst's reaction to the patient unduly influences the patient's transference, the risk is that of transforming the therapeutic relationship into a *folie à deux*.

Racker states that in the countertransference situation the analyst's introjected objects may be transferred onto the patient, creating impediments to analytic work. If, for example, the analyst's need to be loved is thwarted, and he senses the patient's resistance as an expression of hatred, his capacity for objectivity may be distorted, provoking associations or images of archaic objects. In his later paper (1957) however, Racker emphasises that these images and associations, particularly those reactions of great intensity, are nonetheless, revealing of otherwise hidden dynamics and expressive of the analyst's identification with the patient's internal objects. Specifically, he enumerates:

> 1. Countertransference reactions of great intensity, even pathological ones, should also serve as tools. 2. Countertransference is the expression of the analyst's identification with the internal objects of the analysand, as well as with his id and ego, and may be used as such. 3. Countertransference reactions have specific characteristics (specific contents, anxieties, and mechanisms) from which we may draw conclusions about the specific character of the psychological happenings in the patient.
>
> (305–306)

These observations are significant with regard to my understanding regarding the sources, construction and uses of the visual and imagistic aspects of the analyst's countertransference, which I discuss more fully in the next two chapters. In considering the impact of the countertransference on the analyst's capacity to function, Racker is influenced by Helene Deutsch (1934) who recognises two distinct processes: the first being the analyst's identification with aspects of the patient's ego (such as impulses and defences) and the second, which Deutsch describes as 'the "complementary position", or the identification with the patient's images (according to the phantasies of transference)'. I extend this idea to include countertransference imagery, properly processed, as being potentially equally instrumental in revealing aspects of the patient's internal world.

A further important distinction Racker makes is between, on the one hand *concordant*, or empathic countertransference, whereby the therapist identifies with the position of the patient – a direct form of empathy – and on the other hand, *complementary* countertransference, whereby the therapist identifies with the patient's internalised or transference object(s), while the patient re-experiences the original emotion, but now in the presence of the analyst.

The therapist's experience may thus, be a source of emotionally reliable information about the patient's internal landscape and object relations, with concordant identifications yielding information about the self-experience of the patient, and complementary identifications or reactions yielding information about the patient's experience of his objects. This distinction is useful in helping to note and assess the source and meaning of spontaneously arising imagery, when 'scanned' or re-viewed more conscientiously.

Projective and introjective processes in the countertransference

The analyst may also fluctuate between the two positions – positions that accord with the two forms of projective identification: one where the analyst is cast in the role of the patient's object(s), and the other, where the analyst is identified with the psychological and emotional position or experience of the patient. Examples of these two positions, respectively, that include processing through the therapist's visualisation and subsequent reflection, may help to clarify this distinction, as well as some of the other points touched on above.

Clinical example: Mr. C

Mr. C's main symptoms took the form of somatising his feelings, with ailments located in various parts of his body that we had over time come to understand as both an attack upon, and a defence against, a mother internalised as one who possessed and controlled his body and all its functions. Those close to him found this passive form of aggression exasperating, and the frequent somatisation and related hypochondria put a considerable strain on his relationships. Both of these reactions found their counterpart in the clinical setting, as Mr. C appeared to 'work hard' in the therapy, while simultaneously making considerable, albeit unconscious, attempts to frustrate and divert the therapeutic process, yet at the same time feeling aggrieved that his efforts were not appreciated.

The detail I describe took place during a session in which Mr. C described, yet again, how, due to the sudden onset of one of his ailments, an event that had been planned for some time had to be cancelled, letting others down, leaving them feeling put out, disappointed and angry with him. In the session, his associations led to memories of earlier minor illnesses that had had a similar effect of spoiling or delaying plans where there, too, he could not understand everyone being so unreasonably and unfairly exasperated with him, since being ill wasn't his fault. I was aware as he was speaking that, I was fully able to understand the irritation of his friends and family, as I was experiencing something similar in myself while listening to this very familiar grievance.

While he was speaking, I began to notice that I had for some time had in my mind what appeared to be an entirely irrelevant image of a shed in the playground opposite a school I'd attended, around the age of 11 or 12. The scene was not one that I could recall ever coming consciously to mind in the intervening years, but which I found nonetheless, readily recognisable. It had no apparent connection to what was happening in the session. While not exactly intrusive, it remained in my mind in a somewhat insistent way, so eventually, instead of trying to ignore it, I began to wonder why it was there.

What trickled into my mind was a recollection of being part of a group of classmates who were standing behind the shed during a school recess one cold winter afternoon, irritated with a boy from a grade below, someone who I now understand was probably somewhat autistic, who was always regarded as 'odd' and the subject of considerable teasing. He was disturbed to see that some of the boys were passing around a cigarette, smoking, which was of course forbidden. This agitated him, and he told the group that he was going to 'tell the Head-mistress'. In my being aligned with the group who was irritated with the 'out-sider' who was now spoiling the fun and possibly getting us all into trouble, I recognised that this feeling corresponded with my present countertransference response to the patient, and realised – to my surprise and concern – that I had been feeling sympathetic with the group who was irritated with him. That is to

Figure 3.1 Behind the shed.
Source: F. Carey.

say, I saw that I was feeling aligned with his object, rather than with my patient – a form of complementary countertransference, to use Racker's term. In recognising this, I became more immediately in touch with my patient's position. Like the boy in the memory of the scene at the shed, he felt he was doing nothing wrong, quite the opposite. Why was everyone attacking him? While I, on the 'inside', could only see someone who 'didn't get it', and whose inability to connect with others was not only a nuisance, but a threat (if he were to report the smoking).

At the time, in the session, I was able to use the experience of feeling aligned with the object to better understand how this felt to my patient. After the session, as I began to sketch on paper the scene that had been in my mind (Figure 3.1), other thoughts began to emerge. I recognised that at the time of the incident behind the shed, I did in fact have *mixed* feelings about what was happening. My classmates had of course been smoking, but in an effort to head off trouble, they tried to persuade the rather unworldly boy – quite condescendingly – that, being a cold winter day, he had mistaken frosty breath for cigarette smoke and they had just been pretending to smoke what was in fact a cigarette-shaped sweet. It was clear from his reaction that he was sceptical about this explanation, but was really not sure, making himself into even more of an object of derision and ridicule. That moment had registered with me, even at the time, as something about which I felt uncomfortable. And it was that moment of having abused his naiveté that was the source of my own internal conflict in that I had identified with the aggressor in humiliating someone who was more vulnerable than me.

It was this aspect of the image of the shed, and its associated memory, that brought me closer to my patient's actual experience and thereby, to greater understanding of his need to project painful feelings. This led to a circularity of anger and guilt, as it was precisely guilt, entirely misplaced, regarding an early tragedy for which he nonetheless, felt responsible that was at the heart of his own inner conflict. Something had happened in his infancy, which could not possibly have been his fault, but which he attributed irrationally to his own selfishness. As an adult, he of course understood he could not actually have been responsible for what had happened. However, he continued to feel not only that he was to blame, but also that he was being held accountable by others, suffering two conflicting sets of feelings at one and the same time (and in his case, all the time): an unbearable sense of guilt for which he could not forgive himself and, simultaneously, an intolerable sense of injustice, for which he could not forgive others.

The image of the shed, however incongruous in relation to my patient's narrative (which it certainly was), put me in touch with conflictual feelings of my own (irritation and guilt) that seemed aligned to his, as well as those he projected into his objects. He was in a perpetual state of conflict, attacking himself, at the same time as protesting his innocence. So he now continually, unconsciously, recreated situations that would bring both these irreconcilable positions into everyday life, where they would be enacted, either within himself – creating a state of near paralysis – or with others who would be cast in the role of either unjust aggressor, or baffled victim of his passive aggression. His skill in projecting this mix of feelings into others made him into their, and indeed his own, perpetual scapegoat. Unable to face the reality and the pain of what had happened, and mourn what had been lost, he would instead wallow in a sense of grievance (rather than grief) repeating the cycle of guilt and righteous indignation arising from an injustice.

It was the impact of actually seeing my place in that alignment – through the scene behind the playground shed – that helped me to understand the intensity of such irreconcilable feelings that induced the masochistic behaviour, which provoked a form of sadism in his objects, and in effect, getting those around him to take on this persecutory role, to punish him.[3] As I hope I have made clear, the associations here were entirely my own, but they seem to have been stimulated or evoked by my patient's emotional dilemma.

Clinical example: Mrs. D

Mrs. D, by contrast, would barely speak and seemed hostile in her silence, but could not or would not, say how she was feeling, or what she was thinking. From time to time I would become aware that her breathing was noticeable, uneven, her eyes closed, as if she were dreaming. When she did speak, her voice was controlled, her language precise but spare. Although I did not find the sessions particularly uncomfortable, I began to feel quite despairing of my ability to help make sense of either the speech or the silence. However, she came regularly and on time, and seemed to use the sessions, although almost privately, as if I weren't there. On those occasions when Mrs. D did speak, it seemed she wanted to work something out on her own, and I felt redundant to the process. If I commented on either her silence or on what she had said, it was often met with further silence or irritation, as if I were needlessly and pointlessly interrupting a private train of thought. This began to feel, if not intimidating, then certainly inhibiting. During one such lengthy silence, towards the end of the session, I began to notice that I had had in my mind for some time – and not, I realised, just in this session, but only with this patient – an image of a hallway off the entrance to a house, with a staircase to one side. There was nothing remarkable about the scene, and would have been a plan common to the entrance areas of many homes familiar to me from my childhood. However, on this occasion, I noticed that the house was, or was very similar to, the house of a school friend that I used to visit. I remembered that we would enjoy hiding together in the cupboard beneath the stairs, just big enough for the two of us, while the child minder – who never discovered where we were – would grow frantic looking for us, and we would then appear somewhere else in the house, pretending to wonder what all the fuss was about. While musing on this memory, quite unexpectedly, I began to feel slightly breathless. The room was still very quiet, I was sitting slightly behind and to one side of the couch where the patient was lying on her back, turned slightly away from me. For a few moments, I began to wonder if this is what a panic attack feels like, something I had never experienced before and certainly never in a session, verging on a wish to stand up and walk out of the room, and escape. Then, with some effort, I was able to take a few deep quiet breaths, and regained my composure.

While discussing what had happened in supervision, I remembered something about the cupboard under the stairs that I had hitherto forgotten, which was that the friend whose house it was had once told me about locking her little brother there when her parents weren't around and terrifying him with threats of leaving him there until he suffocated and no one would ever find him. When I asked her about being frightened that he would tell their parents about what she had done, she said that he would never do that because she would simply deny it, and nobody would believe him. (We were about nine or ten at the time, although I think she may have been talking about an even earlier time in their lives).

I was somewhat apprehensive about seeing my patient the following day, concerned that I might find myself in the same anxious state. Although this did not happen, I was very aware of the way I'd felt the day before and, during another lengthy, somewhat rigid silence, I said, 'You seem almost afraid to speak', to which Mrs. D unhesitatingly replied, 'I'm terrified all the time. I'm terrified if I speak, and I'm terrified if I don't speak.' She then did, eventually, speak about having been abused by a neighbour, a young man who would regularly babysit for the family. He would take her into the cupboard in her bedroom, hold his hand over her mouth while the abuse took place, and then tell her that what happened was a secret, and that there was no point in telling anyone as no one would believe her, because he was a trusted friend of the family.

Quite how that particular image came to my mind is difficult to say, other than perhaps through the occasional stifled breathing that I could sense in the patient, the habit of seeming to start speaking, then stopping herself before she began (which happened often), certainly her palpable apprehension, the lack of trust alongside the need to trust; the fear, or the conviction, that trust would be betrayed. Certainly, the image did not arise suddenly in my mind; it seemed to emerge gradually, like a slowly developing photograph, just shadows and smears before a recognisable picture begins to take shape. However it came about, the image that did eventually appear in my mind, and the subsequent associations, enabled me to register the patient's inhibiting fear. The intensity of the feeling that took me by surprise, effectively paralysing me, eventually helped me to connect with something of the nature and complexity of Mrs. D's silence, the caution with which she spoke, the depth of her fear, and her mistrust of those who were there to protect her.

So, while the specific character of the visual countertransference may indeed arise out of the analyst's own internal, at times conflictual, experiences and attendant associations, it is often stimulated by the patient's presence, or their 'material', and may be of singular value in understanding their internal world. Racker's central thesis, that the therapist's emotional responses specifically reflect the psychic position of the patient, and provide him with an accurate and current emotional map thereto, comprehensively represented the shift then taking place in the perception of the analyst as detached and neutral, towards one more emotionally affected by and engaged with the events of the consulting room.

Of significance with regard to later comments concerning hypnagogic states (see Chapter 4), Racker then says something interesting about the role that *distraction* plays in making oneself aware of the countertransference, namely (and following Ferenczi [1927]), that the analyst's distractibility is a reflection of the patient's resistance, a form of mutual withdrawal, which is itself a response to the 'imagined or real psychological position of the analyst' (Racker 1957:317). Ferenczi suggests that 'if the analyst has withdrawn, is not listening, but thinking of something else', and, I would add, imagining, fantasying or picturing something, 'this event may be utilized in the service of the analysis like any other information'; and furthermore, the guilt that the analyst may feel over such a withdrawal 'is just as utilizable analytically as any other countertransference reaction' (ibid.).

Racker also stresses the importance of paying equal attention to such distracted thoughts as he would to the free associations of the patient. Significantly, he refers to 'the manifest picture in the patient', or 'object imagoes', which he suggests communicate a sense of the patient's state of mind to the analyst, enabling him to 'deduce from each of his countertransference sensations a certain transference situation' (ibid.:347). In speaking of 'object imagoes', Racker is referring to an idea that was introduced through the writings of Carl Jung, then developed by Melanie Klein and her followers (notably, Susan Isaacs) to convey the idea of complex and powerful figures such as the combined parent figures as perceived by the infant, derived from, but more numinous than, the everyday experience of these two individuals. The imago implies an idea of the mythical or charismatic, so it is the introjected image of the object(s) that incorporates their actual or fantasied attributes, and supplies the template for the super-ego. Susan Isaacs (1948) writes:

> In psycho-analytic thought, we have heard more of 'imago' than of image. The distinctions between an 'imago' and an 'image' might be summarized as: (a) 'imago' refers to an unconscious image; (b) 'imago' usually refers to a person or part of a person, the earliest objects, whilst 'image' may be of any object or situation, human or otherwise; and (c) 'imago' includes all the somatic and emotional elements in the subject's relation to the imaged person, the bodily links in unconscious phantasy with the id, the phantasy of incorporation which underlies the process of introjection; whereas in the 'image' the somatic and much of the emotional elements are largely repressed.
>
> (93)

Racker's use of the term 'imago' is clearly not literally a reference to the patient's verbal descriptions of 'pictures', and the clear implication here is that the analyst has perceived such pictures or imagos[4] as projections, in order to be able to speak of them as 'manifest' in the patient. He states that the analyst's feeling about the patient at such moments of communication of the internal imago adds a dimension of understanding to the patient's internal state, and the character of the transference. Equally worth noting is that an awareness of an *absence* in the patient's picture of his internal world may enable an under-standing of a *defence* against certain object imagos, such as persecutory, tantalis-ing, sadistic or vindictive objects, and it may be that the analyst is given the task of carrying these on the patient's behalf.

It is possible that where there is an unusual abundance, or type, of imagery occurring with a particular patient, this may indicate a form of resistance whereby the patient is unable to bring something into consciousness, and this becomes the task of the therapist. Notwithstanding, Racker cautions that 'hunches' need to be tested through self-analysis and further listening: an obvious, but necessary caveat against 'wild analysis'. It seems to me self-evident, however, that the therapist would be able to test the validity of an inter-pretation that arises out of spontaneous imagery in the same way as that which arises out of any other response – tentatively, as a possibility, without imposing a premature conclusion.

Roger Money-Kyrle (1956) speculates, in a footnote, how a patient manages to impose a fantasy and related feelings upon the analyst, thereby denying it in himself. He naturally dismisses the idea of extrasensory processes, but believes such communications arise out of archaic, pre-verbal experience that appears not to have come from the patient at all. 'The analyst experiences the affect [and I would include "image"] as being his own response to something' (366).

In a major critical review of countertransference, Otto Kernberg (1965) also comments on the role of projective identification in ego identity, which con-tributes to the character of the countertransference, in that the anxiety that pro-voked the projection gives rise to a defensive need to control the object, with a consequent blurring or fusing of ego and object. In the process, the therapist's own anxieties that are connected to early – particularly aggressive – impulses may be activated, which may now be directed towards the patient. While risky, nevertheless:

> the emotional experience of the analyst at that point … may provide information of the kind of fear the patient is undergoing at that time and of the fantasies connected with it, because this process in the analyst has come about by "duplicating" a process in the patient.
>
> (47)

Something of this dynamic is evident in the example of Mrs. D (see p. 41).

In the following decade, Greenson (1974) extended the debate between the 'classic' or solely transference-induced, and the 'totalistic' positions, noting that the conditions of analysis expose the analyst to the patient's full range of loving and hateful feelings, provoking countertransference reactions that could interfere with the working alliance. However, he also cautions that sustaining the neutral position may become an unconscious defence against more spontaneous loving or hateful responses to primitive stimuli. This caution against over-defensiveness can equally be applied to imagery that arises spontaneously, particularly where it is felt to derive from earlier and more primitive, less well-defended or less sophisticated sources than the sites of language. This defence is further reinforced by virtue of the difficulty inherent in the communication of imagistic ideas that results in resorting to language, and thereby, possibly detaching from the affective, perhaps uncomfortable, source of the thought. I discuss the relative positions of defensive flight to and from imagery and verbal articulation more fully further on.

Co-construction

At about the same time, Joseph Sandler, writing on role-responsiveness (1976), discussed the impact and influence of the person of the analyst on the patient's internal processes, discovered through monitoring the analyst's mental associations while listening to the patient. Here, the risks of over-identification or enactment are mitigated through the filters of free-floating attention and what Sandler describes as 'free-floating responsiveness', or 'the capacity to allow all sorts of thoughts, daydreams and associations to enter the analyst's consciousness while he is at the same time listening to and observing the patient' (44). Sandler describes intrapsychic role-relationships whereby the patient casts himself and the analyst in complementary roles, and the patient's unconscious wishes 'are expressed intrapsychically in (descriptively) unconscious images or fantasies, in which both self and object are represented in particular roles', and 'Our clues ... to the unconscious inner role-relationship which the patient is trying to impose, come to us via our perceptions' – which I understand to include visualisations – 'and the application of our analytic tools' (45).

In a paper on the clinical use of reverie, Charles Spezzano (2001) offers the following example of a relatively conscious use of empathic imaging to gain hitherto elusive insight into the emotional state of his patient, a middle-aged woman who:

> mentioned that one of her children had complained about her wearing too much perfume. In the reverie that followed, I imagined, through a series of images (resembling film-clips more than photographs), about women asking their husbands or lovers if they were wearing the right amount of perfume. I wondered if my patient believed the question of how much perfume was enough had to be answered by a man. So I said, "You have no man to ask?" She said "No", and I said she wanted me to tell her. It didn't count when children told her. I wondered, I told her, when I came into the building and could tell she was there already, because I could smell her perfume while

climbing the stairs, if she was trying to tell me something. She thought now that it had been a message: "This is what it is like to be a middle-aged woman with no man." I had not been understanding, I was then able to say, of how profoundly alone she felt without a man to relate to her body, and she replied that it is like being invisible, undetectable by any of the senses, passing through the world of men like a ghost. "A vapor", I said, and we knew together that the vapor of perfume was an announcement of her ghost-like sense of herself'

(556–557)

Christopher Bollas (1983) distinguishes between the 'direct' and 'indirect' countertransference, similarly related to each other in the manner of Racker's 'concordant' and 'complementary' positions. He suggests that the patient's free associative process takes place partially within the analyst, and regards such responses that may be described as 'hunches' as informing the analyst of 'true self activity' in the patient. Such responses, based on non-instinctual sensing, he calls 'indirect use of the countertransference', a condition similar to that of the mother who explores her feelings and perceptions to discern her baby's needs in the absence of language. Bollas contrasts this with 'direct countertransference': the analyst's direct experience of the patient's person or material (11).

He maintains that through the process of projective identification patients recreate their infantile life in the transference in such a way as to compel the analyst to relive elements of it through the countertransference, thereby learning how it felt for the patient to be the child of such a parent – or how the analyst becomes the patient's 'transformational object' (Bollas 1979). Referring to Winnicott's (1971) concept of 'potential space', Bollas regards the psychoanalyst's mental neutrality as a form of 'internal potential space' (Bollas 1983:3) that functions – to use Milner's term (1952, and see p. 25) – as a frame or, in Lewin's (1946) terms as a 'dream screen'. This heightened sensibility in the analyst alerts him to 'hunches, feeling states, passing images, fantasies and imagined interpretive interventions', suggesting that in this way the analyst can find the patient within himself (Bollas 1983:3). This can be accomplished by 'creating an internal space which allows for more complete and articulate expression of the patient's transference speech' than were he to adhere to a 'notion of absolute mental neutrality' (Bollas 1983:3–4). He thus, sees the function of the analytic space as facilitating regressive elements not only in the patient, but in the analyst too, a state that he calls 'countertransference readiness' (Bollas 1983:2–3). I suggest that this state of readiness includes a capacity to notice and make use of the images that may flow spontaneously into this space.

Wolstein (1975) speaks of the 'principle of psychic symmetry' to describe the manner in which both transference and countertransference are jointly constructed. As the transference is not exclusively patient-centred, neither is the countertransference exclusively analyst-centred, 'the unconscious aspects of the analyst's countertransference [being] greatly involved in the therapeutic experience' (78–79).

In an influential paper on countertransference, Denis Carpy (1989) speaks about the patient who evokes intense feelings in the analyst, and comments that whatever the continuing debates about what constitutes, and what is of value in the countertransference, what has become clear to him is that the experience is co-constructed. He maintains that the patient plays a dynamic role in the analyst's countertransference, specifically referring to the patient's ability 'to induce in the analyst a state of mind very similar to one he is attempting to eliminate in himself', mainly through projective identification. Carpy situates the containment function of the analyst alongside the power of projective identification, to affect the recipient in such a way as to 'experience whatever is projected into him' (288), reinforcing a growing understanding of the therapist's countertransference as partly constructed by the patient. He suggests that the 'inevitable' partial acting out of the countertransference allows the patient to see the impact of his projection upon the other, the analyst, who struggles silently with it. This process contributes, possibly more than the interpretation itself, to psychic structural change much as the maternal reverie helps to transform the infant's anxiety into something tolerable.

Use of countertransference imagery

Continuing the theme of 'non-verbal interaction', Theodore Jacobs (1993), through the presentation of a single analytic hour – in which he acknowledges that he will probably be telling more than the reader cares to know about the contents of the writer's imagination – closely tracks the often unremarked, imagistic experiences that arise in his mind during the session that gradually emerge from the mutual seemingly random contributions of the two participants' psyches acting upon each other. It is unusual to have such a vivid published account of the imagery that comes to the mind of the therapist throughout the session, and the use he makes of it, so it is worth following some of that detail here.

The patient, Mr. V., is a 38-year-old attorney, very presentable, judgemental, someone with whom it can be difficult to either sympathise or empathise, 'whose bland exterior conceals a streak of violence' and about whom there is 'something menacing'. On the morning of the session in question, the analyst is feeling tense in his new office, which he expects to be sneeringly criticised by the patient. When he hears the patient coming, the analyst finds himself fussing over arrangements in his new consulting room and:

> As I do so the image of a writer I have studied with suddenly appears in my mind [who] confessed to a daily ritual.... Before he can settle down to write, and as a way of avoiding this task, he dutifully sharpens half a dozen pencils and lines them up, one by one, on his desk. I realise that this thought has come to mind because I am delaying going to the door. When I do so, I am about thirty seconds late.
>
> (Jacobs 1993:9)

Then, while sitting with the patient, the analyst is reminded of his feelings for both his father and his own therapist, both of whom he regarded as more like the patient: ambitious; exacting; demanding; competitive; critical; and both very unlike himself. The image of his father appears in his mind, on the telephone, shouting at an employee. As he imagines this, he feels:

> the same kind of anxiety that as a child I experienced when, lying in bed, I overheard my father flying into a rage. I then recall how, through my analysis, I was able, in large measure, to overcome my fear of him. I am aware that I am having this thought as a way of saying that I can deal with Mr. V and with whatever feelings he evokes in me.
>
> (Ibid.)

The ensuing exchanges, often very uncomfortable for the analyst, develop the theme of defences against unconscious envy that the patient recognises and to which he is able to associate with memories of envy of his bullying older brother. Jacobs continues, 'As Mr V recounts this story I have a mental picture of his brother; tough, mean-spirited, nasty, and I feel rage at this brutish fellow. Then suddenly I recall my own childhood experiences of being bullied' by gangs who would attack Jewish kids in the neighbourhood, stealing their possessions and often beating them up. Jacobs recounts how he hated those bullies and realises that he has associated Mr V's brother with them. 'I warn myself to be alert to the dangers involved in doing so and identifying with my patient as the victim of brutality' (10).

Mr. V then moves seamlessly from the theme of envy to that of disdain, particularly for his brother's new found religiosity, which he believes has influenced a mutual acquaintance whose home Mr. V describes, cynically, as being packed with valuable religious artefacts. A number of images arise in the analyst's mind, one being that of a former supervisor whose interest in subliminal perception influenced Jacobs, then, 'At that point another puzzling memory surfaces. I recall my grandparents' apartment ... I picture its front door. Clearly displayed on it is a mezuzah [a Jewish symbol attached to the doorpost].' Then another image arises. He pictures the front door of the new office and recalls that a mezuzah is also affixed to it, but has been all but obscured by successive coats of paint. He had noticed it but then forgot about it 'quite completely'. He wonders how he has got distracted by these thoughts and images when it occurs to him that probably, subliminally, his patient has also seen this almost invisible sign on the door. The therapist asks Mr. V if he has noticed anything on his way in on this, his first visit to the new building. Mr. V asks if he is referring to 'one of those Jewish things on your door?' The exchange leads to Mr. V's sensitivity about being Jewish, particularly in his professional life. The therapist silently recognises that this has been an issue for him, too, at many different times of his life (including the bullying that occurred when he was a boy).

Further images arise in this way throughout the hour, leading the therapist – through his countertransference associations – gradually to be able to link aspects of the patient's past with his own, and with the patient's current concerns including envy, fraudulence, fear, castration, anxiety, rivalry and shame. Jacobs cautions that although not all such material is of equal value, nonetheless:

> when our ears are properly attuned and we are listening well, the shards of memory and imagination that arise from within constitute meaningful and often illuminating responses to our patients' communications. Such experiences have taught us that our ability to understand another person depends on our capacity, not only to listen to that individual, but to ourselves as well.
>
> (14)

To this end, the analytic process depends 'on the working through of resistances in the analyst as well as the patient' (7), through paying attention to the therapist's thoughts, feelings, images, fantasies and physical sensations that arise in response to unconscious communications from the patient.

Jacobs's work had an impact on Norbert Freedman (1997) who carried out a study filming practitioners at work with more or less 'difficult' patients where he analyses the striking video evidence demonstrating the analysts' non-verbal reactions to the patient to discern the boundaries between empathy, and constructive and destructive forms of countertransference. The gradual emergence of a recognition of the complex contribution that countertransference makes to the analytic process corresponds to the equally measured understanding of the unfolding of the mechanism of projective identification. The analyst appears not only to receive and contain the patient's transference, but also discovers correlative responses from within his own psyche and emotional experience.

Freedman (1997) states that for the countertransference to function productively, the analyst must be able to retain an inner psychic space to sustain the symbolising function, even in the face of intense feelings and fantasies stimulated by the experience of being with the patient. This requires a capacity for empathy without being overwhelmed, a form of 'vicarious participation' that enables the analyst to create 'a parallel affective and imagistic scenario that resonates with the patient's, while sustaining a thin, permeable boundary between that evoked scenario and the intrusion of highly personal interferences' (82). He suggests that it is possible, in fact necessary, 'to distinguish between the constituents of empathy, useful countertransference, and countertransference that is destructive of the treatment process' (ibid.) – a capacity discovered through analytic listening. Freedman states that, just as for the patient, symbolising requires the creation of 'representational space', and that 'such space-creating activity becomes even more imperative for the listening analyst' (ibid.).

He observes the similarity between Jacobs's description of the free-floating process, and the kinesic patterns recorded during the taped observations of his own research. He finds in Jacobs's account a 'three-dimensional listening space' indicative of his capacity to 'resonate' with the patient, and at the same time engage in inner dialogue, towards the task of interpretation (98). This model of listening involves both taking in the patient's psychic reality based on mirroring, alongside an internal dialogue, listening to both the patient and oneself, simultaneously, the 'oscillating attentional perspective' that Freedman describes as the 'symbolizing countertransference'. This concept of the 'three-dimensional listening space' and the representational space, are closely linked to my own argument for a space – or the nurturing of a space – that enables a generative capacity for associative imagery.

Staying with the idea of symbolising, Thomas Ogden (1994) writes:

> a major dimension of the analyst's psychological life in the consulting room with the patient takes the form of reverie concerning the ordinary, everyday details of his own life ... not simply reflections of inattentiveness, narcissistic self-involvement, unresolved emotional conflict, and the like; rather, this psychological activity represents symbolic and proto-symbolic (sensation-based) forms given to the unarticulated (and often not yet felt) experience of the analysand as they are taking form in the intersubjectivity of the analytic pair.
>
> (12)

Phillips (2002) extends Ogden's 'reverie' to include an intersubjective reflection of the patient's disavowed states based on the incidence of uncannily similar material within both the form and content of his own imagery and silent fantasies, alongside the patient's verbal discourse.

Richard Lasky (2002) disputes that countertransference is a value-free concept and seeks to clarify terms by differentiating first between the 'analytic instrument' – as he defines the inner states of the analyst – and more general behaviour in the session. He takes Freud's idea of 'empathic attunement', where the analyst turns 'his own unconscious like a receptive organ towards the transmitting unconscious of the patient ...' as his model of practice (Freud 1912:115–116) employing the term 'analytic instrument' to define the constructive work of the analyst's unconscious, since he believes Freud's original term is now unhelpfully at variance with much common current usage. He adds that the (facilitating) analytic instrument should *not* be seen as a form of projective identification, which is a defensive operation that may contribute to the functioning of the analytic instrument, but is not the equivalent of it. It is but one component alongside numerous others, such as 'direct identifications, complementary identifications, concordant identifications, disidentifications, counteridentifications, projective counteridentifications, ego identifications, and superego identifications' all of which affect the analyst's internal picture of the patient along with such other processes as transference distortions, objective reality, internal conflicts, personal defence, blind spots, etc. (Lasky 2002:72).

While I accept the argument with regard to the need for clarification of terms, and recognise the risk of ambiguity, confusion and internal contradiction in a term as broad as 'countertransference', nonetheless, I see no need here for the adoption of further neologisms or phrases, since it will be clear by now that for the purposes of my argument, at least, the countertransference refers to the analyst's or therapist's internally developing (on a 'sliding scale' of consciousness) emotional response to the patient, and it is more useful to discern what is happening in that countertransference, whether it is concordant or complementary, for example, whether it is defensive or empathic, to establish its role within the session. And for that, all that is needed is a suitable adjective.

Here, I am particularly interested in countertransference responses such as those previously alluded to in Bollas's paper (1983) as 'hunches, feeling states, passing images', mental responses that may come 'out of the blue' or, conversely, surprise us with the discovery that something that may have been lurking in the shadows of the work with a patient, will stealthily drift – or suddenly erupt – into consciousness; ideas or feelings to which we may have become habituated, such that they have become almost invisible, until we eventually yield to their demand for interpretative attention.

Visual reverie

In discussing the experience of visual reverie, I draw on two papers on the theme by Thomas Ogden, both written in 1997, one mainly on its use in interpretation (1997a) and the other (1997b) mainly on its relation to metaphor. Both papers speak of the analyst's reverie experience as an 'indispensable avenue to understanding and interpretation of both transference and countertransference' (1997b:721), yet one whose dimensions had (at the time) remained relatively unscrutinised. Importantly, he notes the ease with which reverie may be dismissed as irrelevant, appearing as it does in the most mundane and unremarkable forms. He quotes Randall Jarrell (1955:68) speaking about Robert Frost's poetry, in describing reverie as being about 'people: people working, thinking about things, falling in love, taking naps ... the habit of the world, its strange ordinariness, its ordinary strangeness'. Reverie experience includes 'ruminations, daydreams, fantasies, bodily sensations, fleeting perceptions, images emerging from states of half-sleep ... tunes ... and phrases ... that run through our minds ...' (1997a:568). Ogden notes that it is both a personal and private – at times even embarrassing – event, difficult to share even with oneself, meaning that the attempt to hold onto such thoughts and feelings is to forgo a type of instinctively protected privacy with the consequence that its contents are rarely revealed or questioned. It is, or has been, therefore a phenomenon not often discussed with colleagues or written about, easily dismissed as irrelevant and so, forgotten.

Yet, while private, at the same time the phenomenon has an intersubjective quality. And although these thoughts may not be directly or even consciously shared with the patient, they nonetheless, inform the processes of perception, identification, understanding and interpretation, arising as Ogden believes, not solely from the mind of the therapist, but from what he terms the 'intersubjective analytic third' (Ogden 1994), a form of active, albeit unconscious, co-construction. He paraphrases Winnicott in observing that 'there is no such thing as a patient', apart from the analyst and, continuing with Winnicott's instruction (1971), this paradox is to be accepted, tolerated and respected, 'for it is not to be resolved' (xii). It is also often difficult to 'catch hold' of reverie, even more so perhaps than dreams, as it is not framed in the same way as dreams, but seamlessly, unobtrusively, melts into other psychic states to be 're-claimed' by the unconscious (Ogden 1997a:569).

It is risky to interpret immediately from reverie within the session, since grasping meaning usually requires silent reflection, but the process may be used as an emotional compass that hints usefully at the direction or context of the patient's state of mind at the time or inner world more generally. Ogden observes that the understanding that arises from reverie is usually discovered retrospectively, and it is 'almost always unanticipated' (ibid.). He reminds us of 'the importance of the analyst's close attentiveness to the nuances and details of the events in the analytic hour in the service of drawing inferences and framing interpretations concerning unconscious fantasy, anxiety and defence'. He includes in reverie 'the most mundane, quotidian, unobtrusive thoughts, feelings, fantasies, ruminations, daydreams, bodily sensations and so on that usually feel utterly disconnected from what the patient is saying and doing at the moment' (1997b:721).

Finally, he cautions that these 'loosely knit "excerpts"' from his internal dialogue 'in no sense comprise a comprehensive, balanced statement of a theory of technique' (1997b:719), but rather serve as a guide to what is most alive in the analytic encounter. Mostly, this internal dialogue – to which the patient is an unwitting contributor – takes place at a subliminal, if not actually unconscious, level and comprises fleeting observations, glimpses, glances, images, sounds, flickers, traces that, when taken together, gradually begin to form a composition – music, rather than merely notes.

As an example of both the flavour, as well as the clinical uses of reverie, Ogden (1979a) offers a summary of three consecutive sessions with a middle-aged female patient, that retrospectively track the course of his reverie. Using his examples in a very condensed form, I want to draw attention to the visual elements in his description. These can be vivid, but as he notices, the fluid character of reverie means that they are also difficult to catch hold of, and these elements, more so than the narrative itself, can thereby easily get lost.

In the vignette, the therapist (O) feels tense and a little nauseous at the approach of the anxious and needy Ms. B, in whose presence he feels defensive of his time, space and skill. She seems always to take and take, never feeling she gets, or is given, enough. As Ms. B speaks in a stiff, disjointed, aimless way, O finds himself feeling resentful, withholding, in fact placed precisely in the habitual position of Ms. B's objects. Part of his mind drifts. A scene from a film floats into his mind, in which a corrupt official is ordered by a Mafia boss to kill himself. The hour moves slowly. in a mesmerising way, he mentally synchronises the second hand of a ticking clock with that of a digital clock. He has an image of a friend with a heart condition. O imagines having this condition himself, never waking up from surgery. A profound sense of loneliness and loss overtakes him. The image of a close friend who has recently died of cancer appears. He recalls a last conversation with her in which a false sense of comfort and reassurance distanced them both from the undoubted fact that this was not, and could never be, a shared experience: it was she and she alone whose death was imminent, her fear and loneliness unreachable by friendship or sympathy. Here, there was no such thing as 'we', and the conversation, he now feels, would surely have left his friend feeling even more alone in her isolation.

His patient speaks. The tone feels false. O senses her need to present an idealised picture of herself masking the reality of loneliness and hopelessness of being close to anyone. He thinks about having just been watching the two clocks briefly synchronise, how this may have represented an unconscious effort on his part to create a sense of alignment, knowing this to be false. Ms. B reports a disturbing dream about a man who drops a baby. O senses a flicker of hope. The images of the dream seem to offer them both a more accessible, more truthful language, but the patient retreats.

The chaotic feelings that emerge in this session show up in the next. O's attention once again drifts, watching a play of sunlight on curved glass. The curves seem feminine, like a woman's body. This image in the real world is replaced in his floating attention by an imaginary one of a large stainless steel container in a factory, with details of clanking machinery, as if about to malfunction. He recalls Ms. B's difficulty as an infant in breastfeeding and he experiences a sensuous and sexual aliveness with her (the light playing on the beautifully curved glass), that then turns into something dysfunctional (the malfunctioning machinery), mechanical and harsh. He remembers how Ms. B had arched her back two sessions earlier, in a gestural response to the couch as she lay down, and recognises that the gesture may have been one of unconscious seduction rather than the discomfort as it appeared at the time or perhaps one of seduction *and* discomfort.

She reports another dream, again about a baby, something at first alien, 'How could I have given birth to such a thing?' then 'a little boy with wild curly hair'. O interprets her fear of feeling or letting him feel the love she felt for the child in the dream (a representation of O). Ms. B is able to express her gratitude to O for acknowledging and not throwing away the things that she discards in her fear of valuing anything real and precious (truth) that could be lost, but at the same time this makes her feel anxious and exposed, imagining that O – if he saw her naked – would think her breasts were 'too small'. O is reminded again of the friend, J, who died of cancer – breast cancer – and the agony surrounding her surgery. He experiences a wave of deep love for J together with the deep sorrow of losing her, a range of feeling that had not previously been part of his experience while with Ms. B. The sense of isolation in the session diminished, and something more nuanced took its place enabling the therapist to work more effectively once again.

Bion (1962a) wonders what is required of the mind of the mother, if the infant is to be able to profit from reverie in a manner similar to its ability to profit from the nourishment of the breast. He answers his question by stating that the mother's capacity for reverie and the content of that reverie are inseparable. If the mother's mind is not somehow with her infant or its welfare, this dissociation or detachment is perceived by the infant, and its anxiety (fear of death) cannot then be transformed by 'alpha-function' and falls into the limbo of 'nameless dread'. Bion reserves the term 'reverie':

> only for such content as is suffused with love or hate. Using it in this restricted sense, reverie is that state of mind which is open to the reception of any "objects" from the loved object and is therefore capable of reception of the infant's projective identifications whether they are felt by the infant to be good or bad. In short, reverie is a factor of the mother's alpha-function which is its fundamental source.
>
> (36)

This ability (initially, the mother's) to tolerate the intolerable, enables transformation of anxiety or dread into something manageable – the tolerance itself being a transformative factor in the process. The parallels with the clinical setting are self-evident, including the state of mind of the therapist who may not know at the time whether she is, or is not, in a state of reverie that may benefit the patient. It is not always obvious that the daydream of the therapist is bringing her closer to, or distancing her from, the patient. But awareness, and analysis, of the daydream imagery may provide a clue not only as to whether it is one or the other, but also why it may be so, and further, how it may be used to create a bridge, to transform the intolerable (toxic, chaotic, 'beta-elements') of either, or both, patient and therapist into something reachable.

Grotstein (1981) reinforces this idea, stating:

> In psychoanalytic practice, the analyst uses a reverie, corresponding to Bion's maternal reverie, which allows for the entrance of the projective identifications as countertransference or as projective counter identifications, which can then be prismatically sorted out and lend themselves to effective understanding and ultimately to interpretations.
>
> (515)

Summary

I consider the countertransference to be a form, and a source, of emotional information deriving from the relationship between the patient and the therapist.

It is the task of the therapist to learn to ascertain the nature of the countertransference, and determine whether its meaning may be of use to the patient in the moment, or of use to the therapist's developing understanding of the patient, to be communicated or made use of at an appropriate point at some time in the therapy. In line with Bion's concepts of the use of reverie, I cite clinical descriptions from several sources, including a more detailed example from Thomas Ogden, to illustrate these concepts and processes that emphasise their often visual nature. Since it is true that insight derived from countertransference experience does indeed involve the personal internal world of the therapist, it is worth considering ways of developing an effective means of both noticing, understanding and making use of such material through greater awareness and insight into the role of representational imagery, and this is the focus of the next chapter.

Notes

1 The term is hyphenated in its earliest versions, both as translated from the German, and in original English texts. The first unhyphenated version in the *IJP-A* appears in 1948, in an American article, so it is possible that geography has influenced form. Both are currently in use. I use the unhyphenated form other than when quoting directly from texts that use the hyphenated form in the original.
2 This had already been delivered as a lecture in 1948.
3 Adapted from Carey, F. (2004). Therapy by design: style in the therapeutic encounter. In B. Bishop, A. Foster, J. Klein and V. O'Connell (Eds.). *Elusive Elements in Practice*. Book 3, 51–66.
4 The Oxford Living Dictionary defines 'imago' as: 'An unconscious idealized mental image of someone, especially a parent, which influences a person's behaviour.' (https://en.oxforddictionaries.com/definition/imago)

Chapter 4

Considerations of representability

Visualisation and image construction in reverie, dream and daydream

Thought is after all nothing but the substitute for a hallucinatory wish.

(Freud 1900:567)

Earlier, I referred to dimensionality as a marker of emotional development, specifically with reference to the way that the idea of 'space' is thought about within psychoanalytic theory and practice, then I went on to discuss some of the processes and phenomena of unconscious, intersubjective communication, as a means of both expressing and perceiving that aspect of individual development.

These ideas were reviewed mainly to contextualise and anchor my key theme, which is an enquiry into visualisation and imagery as potential indicators of the nature of the internal world of the patient, and how it may be reflected through the 'daydream', or dreamlike thoughts of the therapist. I continue with the theme of unconscious communication, focusing now on the intra-subjective, or the therapist's image-based communication with herself in the clinical setting.

In the beginning, was the image: the place, and fate, of the visual in psychoanalytic practice

In a paper entitled: *The Nature and Function of Phantasy*, Susan Isaacs (1948:96) argues both that 'Phantasies are not dependent upon words, although they may under certain conditions be capable of expression in words' and further, that: 'The earliest phantasies are experienced in sensations: later they take the form of plastic images and dramatic representations.' So much of the content of the inner world relies on the imagistic experience, yet the place of the visual in psychoanalysis, particularly with regard to practice, is obscured by, amongst other things, the inevitable primacy of the word through which both theory and practice communicate, clinically, academically and professionally. Nevertheless, the centrality of the image is evident in early accounts of case material such as Freud's and Breuer's experiments with hypnosis (Breuer 1893), followed by Freud's 'pressure' technique and, emphatically in, *The Interpretation of Dreams* (Freud 1900). Here, the themes of image formation, and the relationship between images and words, are either explicitly described or otherwise implicit throughout, including Freud's early description of the hallucinatory experience of primary process (177) wherein representation is mainly – although not exclusively – visual and includes processes that are often so rich in imagistic content such as condensation, displacement and overdetermination. The work can be understood, in part, as a study of the transformation of impressions, sensations and feelings into images, and from there into words – with something likely being lost in translation at each remove.

One of Freud's earliest observations, and one that he claims is 'constantly repeated', is found in *Studies on Hysteria* (1893) where he speaks of the patient's spontaneous reproductions. Freud asserts the significance of every reminiscence that emerges during analysis and insists that there is no such thing as an irrelevant 'mnemic image' (295).[1] If a picture persists, then the thought it represents has not been dealt with, whereas, 'an image that has been "talked away" is not seen again' (296). Freud recognised that part of the value of this technique lay in its capacity to detach the patient from conscious attention to his thoughts, and allow for a more spontaneous, less controlled, response. He suggests that the initially strong images disintegrate as they are transformed into more structured language.[2] The compression of ideas inherent in the imagistic 'tell me what you see', recedes as the more linear narrative construction takes shape. Freud describes, for example, a patient with a hysterical symptom (tussis nervosa) who, under the pressure of his hand, recalled that the symptom began with the children of the family burying her aunt's dog. As the narrative progresses, the picture recedes (ibid.:273). The reader, however, is able to sustain and restore the imagery evoked by the words, as images relating to dogs, aunts, children, death, loss and burials form in the mind – all the while, the process of free association unfolding as hinted at in the above statement describing the 'advantage of the procedure' being its detachment from conscious searching.

James Kern (1978), in writing of a phenomenon similar to that which I am discussing here, that is, the spontaneous appearance within the analyst of apparently unrelated visual images as he listens to his patients, speaks of this transformation in psychoanalytic practice from the analyst who would register pictures from the patient's past (perhaps a more passive practice) to one who listened – a somewhat more active process – for the complexes inherent in the 'flow' of 'verbalized associations' (23). Kern asserts that although, since 1900, dream imagery remained an important component in psychoanalysis, interest in the role and significance of visual phenomena did not substantively revive for about 50 years. This renewed interest included a re-examining of the phenomenon of screen memories, in which Freud (1901) suggested that the vivid recollection and description of images of early experience do not provide accurate images of the past, but fragments and compilations, products of defensive processes against unacceptable ideas, memories and unpleasant experiences (Kern 1978:24). This insight into the capacity and tendency to store memory, whether defensively or economically, in this edited, compressed and somewhat distorted 'snapshot' form has a bearing on my understanding of the use of imagery in the analytic session, which I discuss more fully in Chapter 5. First, I review some ideas on the processes of image construction.

Image construction in regressive, hypnagogic and subliminal states

> One shuts one's eyes and hallucinates; one opens them and thinks in words.
>
> (Freud 1895a:339)

Relaxed states

Conditions within the clinical psychoanalytic setting foster hypnagogic states where the mind is, often, in a relaxed or somewhat regressive mode, conducive to the sort of imagery with which I am concerned, that is to say, imagery that is not consciously constructed, or specifically descriptive, but more associative, spontaneous or seemingly incidental. These conditions were found to promote associative processes in the patient, but of course they impact correspondingly upon the therapist as well, whereby conditions that, for the patient, encourage free association, would, for the therapist, foster 'free-floating attention', one that oscillates between attentive and relaxed modes, and shares some – though not all – of the attributes understood by the terms, 'hypnagogic', (or perhaps regressive, when applied to the patient).

In Chapter 2 of *The Interpretation of Dreams* (1900), Freud remarks on the differences in the mental state between internal reflection, which is more intentional and intense, and psychological self-observation, which is more detached. He notes that this more relaxed state of self-observation is similar to that before falling asleep when, due to the critical faculties being relaxed, 'involuntary ideas' emerge, and 'change into visual and acoustic images ...' (Freud 1900:102) or what Bion, several decades on, describes as 'the experience where some idea or pictorial impression floats into the mind unbidden and as a whole' (1988:17). In later editions of Freud's dream book (in 1914), he adds a note on the conditions under which such transformations take place, that apply also to my argument. Specifically, he cites Herbert Silberer's[3] observation of imagery formation in a semi-wakeful state, noting that if attempting to concentrate on some puzzle or problem, the thought eluded him and a picture appeared in its place, which he recognised as a substitute for the elusive thought (Freud 1900:344).

Jean Piaget (1945) describes this combined experience of image formation and free association from the patient's perspective in the relaxed-regressive state, beginning with a gradual relaxation of 'direction' of the thought process, followed by an imperceptible drifting from one idea to another, like daydreaming. 'At the same time', he writes, 'there is a noticeable tendency to visualise rather than to reason. A series of pictures appears, which he watches and describes ...' (182–183).

Max Warren (1961) describes how, around 1896, as the pressure technique gradually gave way to free association and the emphasis shifted from the 'visual to the verbal and from primary process to secondary process' (506), patients were no longer invited to report what they 'saw', but what they 'thought'. Warren suggests that this shift 'from visual to verbal, and from sleep to wakefulness' initiated the decline in the value of visual imagery as a tool in the understanding of resistances. This development also assumes a state of greater wakefulness in the patient than previously, with sleepiness associated more with imagery, and wakefulness associated more with verbalisation, a shift in emphasis from primary to secondary process, with the patient necessarily operating at a less regressed level when communicating through structured language, than through (reporting) images, particularly as Freud's early technique recommended that the patient's eyes were closed. In lamenting the loss of this early element of clinical discovery, Warren writes:

> My interest in the visual image during free association was stimulated by the analysis of a patient whose obvious lapses in verbalization were followed by shifts in the direction and level of thought, which were traced to unverbalised visual images coincident with his pauses and state of autohypnosis. In one instance, the patient, following a long pause in his associations, and a fruitless inquiry into what he might be thinking, was asked whether he saw anything. He immediately described a picture of a prehistoric animal devouring a man. He explained he had not mentioned it because it seemed so strange and out of context.
>
> (508)

Further associations rapidly unlocked and unblocked the hiatus, with the patient moving freely through thoughts, feelings, memories and ideas that had previously been unavailable 'as the patient's ego was occupied with the task of warding off the derivatives of oral instinctual impulses he was experiencing in the transference' (508).

These descriptions echo several in the work of Otto Isakower who, although he wrote very little for publication, has produced substantial and influential research on the mind in hypnagogic states – often associated with the regressive conditions of the clinical setting (1938, 1957). This state gives rise to distinctive processes, including the blurring of different regions of the body, such as between internal and external, including sensations often accompanied by visual images or impressions, and characterised by a gradual shift in the emphasis of ego functions from those dealing with the external world towards those reflecting upon something more within. Isakower reasons that at this level of regression, perceptual processes are much more concerned with the body ego, and the sensual realm (1938:339). Such heightening of body ego function, perhaps similar to the mother's sensitivity to her infant with more than her mind, contributes, I suggest, to informing the therapist of the patient's emotional state, while the therapist is somewhere between the relaxed and the attentive state of evenly hovering attention.

During the late 1950s, Isakower (1963)[4] began to develop his idea of the 'ana-lyzing instrument', describing a regressive state of mind, that functions similarly to that which Bion speaks of in describing the capacity for reverie. For the patient, the equivalent of this state is achieved through the free association that encourages a reduction in the barriers, a temporary 'truce', between primary and secondary process functioning, in which critical faculties are suspended or relaxed, releasing less rational, more imagistic material; for the analyst, a different, but com-plementary, regression is managed through freely-hovering attention. It is in this altered, less topographically defended or compartmentalised state of consciousness – ideally, echoing or attuned to that of the patient – that the 'analyzing instrument' functions to gain access to otherwise guarded areas of memory, thought and feeling. In such conditions, the analyst's response to the patient is likely to be less verbal, closer to the affective content of the material, and more in touch with his own intuitive, sensory – including auditory and visual – cues, connecting inti-mately with the affective experience of the patient: a state, in other words, closer to primary process functioning, for both parties.

Of significance here is Isakower's suggestion that in this state there is an increased likelihood for images to arise in the analyst in response to the material produced by the patient, as discussed previously in Ogden's examples. Even though the associations are the analyst's, these may also be considered as indi-cators of the patient's inner life, a view strongly supported by Lasky (2002) writing on his version of this function – the 'analytic instrument' – who concurs that such images, representations and pictures, while experienced by the analyst, may nonetheless, be stimulated by the patient, and his material (75). Isakower cites Bertram Lewin who comments that this 'level of wakefulness, at which thoughts are no longer represented only in the form of words, but to some extent also in visual form, brings about an increased ambiguity of what is represented …' (Isakower 1963:206). I discuss this ambiguity further in relation to the idea of what I am calling 'daydream-work'.

Bertram Lewin (1968), who also wrote extensively on dream imagery, refers to Freud's recurring spatial metaphor of the supervised space (Freud 1915) and notes the complex vigilance of Freud's 'little watchman', agreeing that the closer we are to a hypnagogic state the greater the tendency for thoughts to occur as visual images; lying on the couch, or sitting nearby in a state of freely-floating attentiveness, are both clearly conducive to such experience, when thoughts or language may be more likely to take imagistic form. Speaking of the patient, he regards this sleepy state as reflective of the cycle of hunger, feeding and satiety, linking the idea of the dream screen to the maternal breast. Lewin is concerned with primitive and archaic images, paying particular attention to what he calls the 'head image', a universal form consisting of, '… the dark, cavernous image that one has about the inside of one's head, the picture we form of it in our mind' (37), which lays the foundation for the first spatial image of the internal self. He describes degrees of vividness of imagery varying from near-hallucinatory to something more 'felt' than seen, more preconscious than conscious and suggests that this subliminal level is the source of the visual metaphors of speech and writing.

Relationship of primary process thinking to imagery

In his exhaustive studies on image formation, Horowitz, (1970, 1972) also notes the general tendency for images, as well as vividness of imagery, to increase as wakefulness decreases. Further, he agrees that images are less susceptible to (or more independent of) both conscious control and censorship than lexical thought. This very quality, however, is double-edged in that images *may* provide a form of retreat or escape from uncomfortable feelings and ideas, but at the same time, in so doing, slip into areas of association that arouse or reconnect with, the very anxiety from which refuge was sought. I discuss this central paradox in greater detail in Chapter 5 ('Dynamics of Imagery').

Horowitz's extensive research reinforces the earlier hypotheses that visual images often occur in the context of primary process, regressive and concretised forms of thought. The frequent concurrence of image form with regressive states, however, leads to an assumption that primary process thought is represented in images and secondary process thought in words, and that imagistic thought is therefore, more primitive than lexical thought. He challenges this assumption, which he regards as being coincidental, rather than characteristic (1972:794).

Horowitz discusses types of image based on levels of vividness, context, interaction with perceptions and content, and refers to the circumstances that increase image formation, which include levels of wakefulness, from wide awake to fast asleep, encompassing fantasy, reverie, daydreaming and dreaming, noting that image formation alters as alertness wanes. This is in agreement with the earlier observations by Silberer (op. cit.) that a combination of drowsiness, and forced thinking, can lead to an '"autosymbolic" phenomenon' (Horowitz 1970:31). This observation is borne out by others, such as Rapaport (1951) who, in his collected records of thoughts from varying levels of wakefulness, noted that reflective self-awareness, effort and logical thinking all decreased while visual imagery increased in frequency and vividness. Horowitz cites ample data from dream observations under controlled conditions, indicating that early evening dreams tend to revolve around day residues, whereas later dreams tend to centre more on childhood and the past. I discuss more fully the role of 'day residue', and other aspects of dream-work, in both the next section (*'Daydream-work'*), and the next chapter (Chapter 5, 'Dynamics of imagery').

Around the same time, engaged in similar areas of research, Arlow (1969) considers the variations of thinking that occur within more or less conscious states, and describes looking both inward and outward. When this is happening simultaneously he describes it as 'fantasy thinking', a continuous process that is consistent with Freud's description of the movement between conscious and preconscious systems (Freud 1925b:231). Arlow questions the nature of the form that unconscious fantasy takes, and concludes that it is primarily visual in nature, and is easily transformed and transformable into visual representations (1969:47). This might take the form of something like a transparent screen upon which internal and external images are projected simultaneously, creating a layered image that hovers between the two principles of mental functioning. Further, due to the affinity between dreaming and other forms of imagistic experience, it is reasonable to assume a link between 'the emergence of daydreams, fantasies, and other regressive, visually experienced phenomena with alterations in the state of consciousness resembling sleep' (ibid.:31–32). He refers also to the intrusive nature of daydreaming upon conscious experience at all levels, and remarks that while the capacity for intense visualisation decreases with age 'at the expense of the pleasure principle', in the analytic situation, free association taps into this 'constantly flowing stream of fantasy activity'. These become visible to the observing analyst in 'fleeting thoughts, misperceptions, illusions, metaphors of speech and action' (ibid.:33–36) and, I would add, both daydreams and screen memories.[5] Here, again, what is true for the patient in free association, would be true for the therapist in a state of free-floating attention as she, too, may tap into a 'constantly flowing stream of fantasy activity'. The point, however, is that even in this state, according to the principles of free association, images that appear random may well be pertinent to the clinical situation.

Staying with the theme of the daydream, I want to consider how it relates to these various forms of hypnagogic states, and particularly to possible similarities of its construction to that of the dream itself, or what Freud refers to as the 'dream-work', a term I am borrowing and adapting here as 'daydream-work', that includes various forms of distortion such as condensation, displacement, overdetermination, secondary revision, 'considerations of representability' and the source of the dream, the 'day residues'. The following is a revision of Freud's idea of the dream-work, the conversion of the dream idea into something tolerable to both the sleeping and the conscious mind, but here seen through the lens of the daydream or reverie.

The daydream-work

Condensation

Condensation operates visually and conceptually in dreams somewhat as both metonymy and synecdoche operate linguistically, where related terms or symbols represent more layered and complex associated ideas. It may take the form of using an attribute of the subject in question, for example 'suit' for business executive or 'skirt' for a woman. It may equally be the use of a composite part to represent the whole, such as 'turf' for horse racing, or where a generic term such as 'palace' refers to the monarch or the royal family, thereby concealing or disguising the specific by the general, or the precise by the oblique. Just as with these figures of speech, condensation fulfils the requirement of dream 'design' for both efficiency on the one hand, camouflage on the other, but also a form of enrichment – a frequent by-product of ambiguity of meaning.

Horowitz (1970) refers to the capacity of visual imagery to compress data, and thus, depict or communicate perceptions of objects in relationships, condensed into a single image. Thus, it may be the case that patients' imagery gradually coalesces into a 'style' of depiction that expresses the nature of their relationship to their internal objects.

Freud (1900) illustrates the idea with his so-called 'specimen' dream, or the dream of 'Irma's Injection' (discussed and 'illustrated' further, below) in which:

> the principle figure ... appeared with the features which were hers in real life, and thus ... represented herself. But the position in which I examined her by the window was derived from someone else.... In so far as Irma appeared to have a diphtheritic membrane, which recalled my anxiety about my eldest daughter, she stood for that child and, behind her, through her possession of the same name as my daughter, was hidden the figure of my patient who succumbed to poisoning ... she turned into another lady whom I had once examined, and, through the same connection, to my wife.
>
> (399)

That is to say, in this iconic example, a single dream figure alludes to (at least) five associated people or ideas. Although the elements share a common characteristic, they may be otherwise quite unrelated, disparate and even contradictory. It is also interesting to note the details of placement in Freud's description, such as the 'position' in which she was examined, 'by the window', and 'behind her' indicating something hidden, or a temporal sequence and so forth, as is almost inevitable in the description of spatial and visual phenomena that contain pertinent details and information that are often ignored, and thereby lost, in the telling or the writing. As we read, or listen, to the account of this dream, we conjure up a very vivid picture, a sort of filmic sequence. It seems to me almost impossible to hear this narrative without conjuring up our own version of the images that were in the mind of the dreamer (see 'The Specimen Dream' p. 74).

Clinical example: Ms. E

An example from a persistent image within the clinical setting may help to illustrate this process of dream construction as it relates to the daydream. Working with a patient I had been seeing twice a week for just over a year, I gradually began to discern that when I was with her (and only when I was with her) I would often have in my mind a particular image of a cityscape that appeared to have been 'collaged' together from familiar fragments that did not quite belong together. The image consisted of a city street that I was able to recognise due to related features, such as a parking lot and a cinema, with which it was easily identified. I was also aware of a bus that would not normally have travelled on that route. And there was a department store that belonged elsewhere, although nearby. So altogether, a form of condensation made up of different, but familiar, elements, but appearing as a unified picture. Everything about the scene was unremarkable, a form of visual 'background noise', whose persistence eventually provoked my curiosity with regard to its associations, which were as follows: The street name had a direct connection to my patient's country of origin. I recognised the bus, from its shape and colour, as the one going in one direction towards the university of the city in question, then in the other direction, back home. Much of the material Ms. E brought related to getting physically as far away from home as possible, which she did initially by leaving home to go to university, but relating everything she thought and did to the oppressive home from which she felt she could never escape. From my 'vantage point', I could see the side entrance of a department store where I once witnessed someone being chased and caught, perhaps for theft or purse-snatching. The patient lived in perpetual fear of being followed, and also of being 'caught', although this was regarding her sexuality, which would not have been acceptable. I then recalled that on the ground floor of that same department store, as a small child, I was once separated from my mother and taken by staff to a reception area where I was told to wait for her who, having so carelessly let go of my hand, I felt sure would now be incapable of knowing how to find me again. Ms. E lived in a persistent state of anxious attachment to her often distracted and ineffectual mother, pushing her away, resenting her for being distant, then pining for her.

Until I paid attention to these associations, all I had seen was an unremarkable townscape that could be anywhere, where I seemed to be randomly positioning my patient. In treating the picture as if it were more like a dream image, I could recognise associations to my own experiences that drew my attention to corresponding aspects of her life, in particular the ambivalent and anxious attachment between mother and child, and its relevance with regard to the transference and countertransference.

Certainly, these were entirely my associations, not hers, and there was nothing magical or 'telepathic' about them but, being mine, they drew my attention to aspects of correspondence with her internal world – otherwise, worlds apart from my own – that had hitherto eluded me, in my more direct associations to her narrative. The image that at first appeared as a single scene came to my mind in the form of something like a snapshot, or sequence of still images that, rather like Freud's specimen dream, contained numerous details that could be brought to life by examining each of them in turn, and whose elements revealed associations that corresponded to aspects of her experience. In other words, it was 'condensed', 'overdetermined', 'displaced' and replete with links that enabled further lines of enquiry to be opened up and explored.

Displacement

Freud points out that elements that stand out in the dream as it is manifest are rarely the most significant in relation to its meaning, but rather, they are a form of 'decoy', in some way connected, but functioning as a type of camouflage or distraction. Here, the core idea that seeks shelter from consciousness is detached from the object, and transferred onto a less contentious object, or context, in accordance with the leniency of a less vigilant censorship. The chain of associations may be logical, linguistic, sound-based, image-based or structured as a composite of conceptual and sensory experience. The function is to distract.

The daydream too may be seen as a form of displacement, insofar as it removes the subject from having to experience the tension or discomfort of the 'here and now', and transfers it elsewhere, at a safer distance from both uncertainty and anxiety. The location of the daydream may entirely camouflage the fact of its similarity with the present situation, and thereby seem a mere distraction. However, this very reduction in 'threat' induces a more relaxed state, liberating a more creative and effective thought process that can in turn stimulate the therapist's own attunement to the patient, via the ensuing associations to the imagery. The example above illustrates displacement with regard, first, to its banality then, its remoteness in time and place to the patient's circumstances. These both served initially to reduce focus, and to some degree, 'concreteness', in the therapist, but then to stimulate associations that could then be tested or considered with regard to the patient's experience.

Overdetermination

Staying with Freud's schema of dream-work functions, 'overdetermination' refers to the apparent multiple sources of a single dream or event, whereby 'each of the elements of the dream's content turns out ... to have been represented in the dream-thoughts[6] many times over' (Freud 1900:283). Overdetermination may thus, be seen in some respects as the obverse of condensation. Whereas condensation may be understood as a form of compression with numerous elements finding expression through a single symbol, overdetermination can be understood as a form of expansion, with a single idea finding several different forms of expression, as with musical variations on a single theme. Another version of this idea would be the instance of a single symptom having various sources, particularly when activated through a second or later provocation.

A common example might be the apparent absence of affect in response to a painful or traumatic event, such as a serious loss, at the time of its happening, only to be overwhelmed with grief by a later, often less personal or meaningful, loss. Freud referred to this phenomenon as *nachträglichkeit* (1897) (literally 'subsequency' or 'afterwardness', but different from 'hindsight') for which there is no precise English equivalent, but is usually translated as 'deferred action' or, following Lacan's French term, '*après coup*'[7] whereby the seed of the symptom is planted through one event, but does not sprout until 'activated' by a later event, sometimes bewilderingly so there may be no obvious link.

Clinical example: Ms. F

An example of the therapist's daydream may illustrate the concept of overdetermination. The patient began the session with her customary lengthy silence, but in what also appeared to be a moody frame of mind. Thinking about this, I remembered that our last session had ended with a sense of frustration due to urgent thoughts and feelings having surfaced, but I could not remember the precise details, other than that further exploration was curtailed due to the ending of the session. Then, in the present session, sitting for some time with the patient's silence, I noticed that I had been visualising, that is to say, more having an image in mind rather than recalling the actual event, of a recent lecture I'd attended in which matters of a professional nature to do with finding ways of mending hitherto irreconcilable differences were being heatedly debated. I was puzzled to find this event occupying the background of my thoughts, and wondered how I might have 'got there' during this session to which there seemed to be no obvious association. So I began tracking the process.

1   Thoughts of this conference reminded me of something I'd heard recently about another organisation, of which I had some professional doubts, that was holding similar complex discussions.
2   The thought of that organisation brought to mind a recent conversation with a colleague – someone connected with that organisation – who had been speaking to me about an interesting, impressive and enviable, development in his work that was taking him abroad …
3   … and would coincidentally enable him to attend his father's 85th birthday – something that I would never be able to do, my own father having died not only at a very much younger age than my colleague's father, but also when I was very much younger than my colleague, and with so much unresolved.
4   This last thought brought me back to my patient, whose last session, I now remembered, ended with being reminded of a particular encounter with her father very shortly before his death, that also remained unresolved due mainly, she maintained, to his emotional inaccessibility.

Each of these strands of thought, I could see, were more or less, that is to say either closely or indirectly, linked (in my mind) to the patient's psychopathology, that we found ourselves returning to through a very restricted, narrow and repeatedly referenced set of memories. All these strands of thought, that began with wondering about her moody silence and drifted, almost imperceptibly in my mind to the 'scene' of the conference, could be traced back – each in its own right – to the central preoccupations of the moment that had to do with these conflictual, quite painful and seemingly unresolvable, feelings. I then was able to remind myself of something I had noted before with this patient that, her moodiness (which could be quite inhibiting) was a defensive strategy that would discourage either of us from coming close to her painful feelings of guilt with regard to her father, matching his emotional inaccessibility with her own (and both transferentially and countertransferentially, placing me in the position of the emotionally inaccessible father). I was then able to draw some of this to her attention and think with her about what it was that had to be kept out of our thoughts and our communication with each other.

The aim of this example is to illustrate that the overdetermination in my daydream was not so much about drawing attention to the patient's internal world – this was an area of conflict with which we were both already very familiar – but in alerting me to my own resistance to recognising the nature of that conflict (including competitiveness, envy, loss, sadness and defensive detachment) perhaps shedding some light on my detaching myself from her moodiness at the start of the session. Defensively, I preferred to think of her as rejecting and critical, resistant to the process of the therapy, rather than to connect with how fearful she was of the painful feelings that the therapy provoked.

It will be seen, however, that all these processes – condensation, displacement and overdetermination – are marked by a complexity or ambiguity, that is the result of the many possible associations that any one image may evoke, a feature of dream-work imagery that I discuss more fully in the next chapter. However, in both dream and daydream, a consequence of this dispersing or diluting effect of overdetermination may be to diminish or devalue the meaning of the detail, or the symbol, in the sense that 'it could mean anything', or the thought could have come from anywhere, and would require too much effort to pursue; or equally, the chain of associations would be so unreliable, and possible interpretations so varied, that they could not be trusted to be meaningful. This is understandably one of the most effective disincentives for the therapist to take his or her daydream seriously, but I think this would be to the detriment of the therapy, in blunting a potentially useful technical tool.

Secondary revision

Secondary revision is essentially a fiction that enables the dreamer to make apparent sense of the (also apparent) nonsense of the dream by providing a linking narrative that gives the dream greater coherence, but in fact, further distorts it by providing cohesion where none may exist. The equivalent in the daydreaming analyst might be a plausible interpretation of the reverie, but it may also be a premature or anxiety-motivated attempt to try and make sense of something that is as yet incomprehensible. As with dreams, when working with daydreams as a route towards understanding, the process benefits from a combination of inspiration tempered by reflection.

Considerations of representability: object and thing representation

Considerations of representability are the means by which dream-thoughts are transformed into visual images, a process to which Freud paid considerable attention. Early on, dating from his monograph, *On Aphasia* (1891), a study of the disturbance of speech or language, Freud distinguishes between word-presentation – that is to say, an idea or mental image associated to a word or verbal stimulus – and thing-presentation – an idea or mental image associated to an actual object; or, between signifier/signified and sign/thing (comparable to Ferdinand de Saussure's[8] distinctions in the field of linguistics and semiotics). Word-presentation is part of secondary process functioning – it is more ego-orientated and applies within language itself – while thing-presentation is more linked to primary process functioning, a less rational (but no less inventive or 'poetic') aspect of mental organisation and applies to the sensory world of actual objects.

Freud (1915) later describes the word's acquisition of meaning through being linked to an 'object' (or 'thing') – presentation', that is itself a composite of sensual elements, effectively, an open and complex chain of associations. The word-presentation, by contrast, is closed, although 'capable of extension'. The closed system of word-presentation is linked to the object-presentation only by its 'sound-image'. He states, 'Among the object-associations, it is the visual ones which stand for the object, in the same kind of way as the sound-image stands for the word' (214).

In his model, the fact that Freud places great emphasis on the theme of presentation suggests the importance he attributed to the way in which an idea is held simultaneously in two different forms or spaces – the word on the one hand, and the 'mnemic image' on the other, with the different perceptions being differently represented. Freud pursued this theme of distinction between word- and thing-presentation, comparing it to the distinction between experience (which may not necessarily be part of consciousness) and that which is expressed in language (which necessarily is), and he was concerned with the clinical consequences arising from this discrepancy.

Further, thing-presentation is not an image analogous to a single flat surface, photograph or photocopy, but rather is layered, inscribed with meaning and association that gives it an enriched value (or is 'cathected', to use Freud's term). Ideas and words represent things that have not just single meanings, but complexity and ambiguity of meaning. Somewhere within that system of memory, sounds, thoughts and words, an image hovers – but it is a composite image, overlaid with singular experiences and associations and, importantly, is specific to its imaginer, dreamer or daydreamer. Once again, this attribute of ambiguity so effectively enables the image to function dynamically, in the service of both defence, but also discovery, which I discuss further in Chapter 5.

Returning now to his theory on the construction of visual memory (1900), Freud cites Fechner's[9] observation on the difference between dreams and 'waking ideational life' with regard to the psychical location of the 'scene of action'. Freud suggests picturing the imaging part of the mind as a compound instrument, whose component parts he describes as 'agencies' or 'systems' and where:

the psychical locality will correspond to a point inside the apparatus at which one of the preliminary stages of an image comes into being ... (occurring) ... in part at ideal points, regions in which no tangible component of the apparatus is situated.

(536)

Here, the 'agencies' stand in a similar regular relation to each other somewhat (but not precisely) as do those of a system of lenses, with a sensory and a motor component at either end, the former to receive perceptions and the latter to generate activity. He illustrates this complex idea with a diagram that shows the 'psychical apparatus' constructed like a system of lenses, with the stimulus entering at one end, and passing through the system where it is received at the other end (538).

Freud further proposes that the trace left in the perceptual system from the stimulus (that is to say, the 'image') be called the 'memory-trace' and that its function is what we call 'memory'. But there is a difficulty here, in that memory describes an object that exists, or an event that has taken place, and must therefore, be represented as fixed, yet at the same time it must also accommodate ongoing 'modification',[10] or updated information. He therefore, assigns these two functions to separate systems: the one at the front to receive perceptual stimuli but retain no memory-trace, while another behind that transforms the stimuli of the first system into 'permanent traces'.

Perceptions are linked in memory primarily by association. If the perceptual system cannot be attributed itself with memory, then it is to be assumed that 'the basis of association lies in the mnemic systems' of which there must be several 'in which one and the same excitation ... leaves a variety of different permanent records', thereby creating a network of complex paths of association in the memory system (539). In this way, Freud constructs a model whereby the imagery that appears in dreams can be understood as a form of regression – a movement backward within the perceptual system.

Here, I am applying this idea also to daydreams, which are similar to dreams insofar as they readily access the range of associations that is held in the so-called 'mnemic system'. Equally, Freud sees non-pathological hallucinations and visions as regressions – that is, 'thoughts transformed into images' – but 'the only thoughts that undergo this transformation are those which are intimately linked with memories that have been suppressed or have remained unconscious' (544) or, I would add, in relation to daydreams, those connected to that range of phenomena described by the term 'screen memory'.

Further considerations of representability: dreams and daydreams

Returning to the dream-work, Freud classifies the most prominent feature of dreams – their images – within the category of 'representability', that is to say the capacity of the dream to transform thoughts into (mainly) visual images. He says: 'Of the various subsidiary thoughts attached to the essential dream-thoughts, those will be preferred which admit of visual representation' (1900:344), and describes the process memorably with the striking image of 'pouring of the content of a thought into another mould' (ibid.).

In transforming dream-thoughts into dream-images the ideas are compressed involving 'a displacement along a chain of associations' the outcome of which may be 'that a single element has its verbal form replaced by another' (1900:339). That form is usually pictorial, or 'a thing that is capable of being represented' (ibid.), that is, a formation that encapsulates a constellation of ideas into a single, or composite, figure. An example of this might be the appearance of a rebus-like image, whose component parts coalesce into an associated thought. For example, a young woman ('Miss') pushing a pram ('Carriage') might signify the idea, 'miscarriage', wherein the words, and the image also have a further resonance insofar as they are related not only by the coincidence of sounds (i.e. 'Miss' and 'carriage' = 'miscarriage'), but in this case also with regard to the theme of ideas to which they refer. It is often the case that such images are 'heard' rather than seen, and it is not until the dream is expressed in verbal terms, or heard by a listener, that such composite dream figures are brought to light. Another example of this puzzle-like mode of expression comes from a patient describing a dream scene in which she was wearing a purple dress. In the dream, she described the image of herself in the purple garment, which I could see in my mind's eye. I commented that perhaps she felt she was 'in violet' ('invio-late') as it seemed to me that the image embodied the idea that she was impregna-ble. This image needed to be spoken out loud to make sense, which it seemed to do in the context of the material of this and other recent sessions.

This process also benefits both condensation and censorship since, the dream-thought being rendered pictorially, it fulfils the numerous demands of the dream for camouflage. 'This is so', Freud states, 'because in every language concrete terms, in consequence of the history of their development, are richer in associ-ations than conceptual ones' (340) or, in common parlance 'a picture is worth more than a thousand words'. This indicates that imagery, being compressed composites, may function not only to provide an economic 'storage system', but also as a defensive retreat in which images whose very details allow simultan-eously for both specificity and ambiguity may offer greater scope for refuge from uncomfortable thoughts than precise verbal articulation, akin to the idea of 'hiding in plain sight'. This is an aspect of imagery that I discuss further in Chapter 5 ('Dynamics of Imagery').

'Las Meninas'

This idea is naturally most convincingly evidenced in the pictorial arts, where a single image conveys a mass of information in an often minimal format such that the single static picture may inform the viewer about the place, the people, their characteristics, their relationship to each other, the mood of the time, the consistencies, the contradictions, what can be said and what is ineffable.

The well-known 17th century painting, *Las Meninas*, one of the most analysed works in western art, serves to illustrate these ideas effectively as its single plane offers endless and fascinating speculation with regard to interpretation and meaning. The work, by the painter to the Spanish Court, Diego Velasquez, was commissioned around 1656 by the reigning monarch of Spain at the time and was originally entitled *The Family of Philip IV*. It has been known, however, since it was catalogued in 1843 by the Prado Museum in Madrid, where it lives, as *Las Meninas* (the 'Maids of Honour') and invites infinite exploration, just as

Figure 4.1 The family of Philip IV or *Las Meninas*, by Diego Velasquez.
Source: courtesy of the Prado Museum, Madrid.

might the sort of significant dream that rewards continued revisiting and discovery of unfolding meaning, as one delves deeper and notices more. As with dreams, the details that reveal themselves on closer observation seem at first to provide answers, but in fact keep on raising questions, drawing the viewer deeper into the folds of the painting. While the subject of the work seems at first obvious, the longer you look, the more intriguing it becomes.

The painting

In this immense and extraordinary work, the figure at the centre of the foreground, and the one that first catches the eye of the viewer, is that of the only surviving child of the royal couple, the five-year-old infanta Margaret Theresa, and it would appear, at first sight, that the artist was commissioned by her parents to capture her in a semblance of informality befitting a child of this age, but that at the same time sets out to convey the fabulously privileged and powerful world of which she is here the centre. She is surrounded by her entourage that includes the two curtseying maids of honour, *Las Meninas*, of the eventual title, two dwarves, a governess dressed in mourning, a bodyguard and a dog. The figure in the background, stepping either into or out of the picture, is the queen's chamberlain. On the same level, visually, on the back wall, we see what appears to be a mirror showing a reflection of two figures, that of the king and queen. Between the back wall and the child, standing to the side, is a self-portrait of the artist, looking out into the space from which the viewer is looking in. So, nine figures of varying stature both actually and compositionally, two reflected figures and a dog.

Whoever or whatever we think may be the actual subject of the painting, spatially, the small 'reflected' double portrait of the royal parents, the king and queen, is at the epicentre of the work. We may therefore, surmise that it is this pair who would be standing where the viewer is, outside the picture plane, gazing into the room, but visible to us only through the reflection in the mirror on the back wall (where we might be able to see ourselves reflected if this were an actual room with an actual mirror on the far wall).

But here, an uncertainty arises: is the reflection we see that of the actual king and queen in the room (but out of the frame), or is it a reflection of a double portrait of the royal couple that is currently being painted on the front of the canvas, of which only the back is visible to us? If so, this pair may be not only doubled up in our minds, but tripled: first, standing, invisibly, in the place of the present viewer; then again – also invisibly – in the possible double portrait that is currently being painted on the canvas on which the artist is now working; and finally, just visible in the mirror's reflection at the far end of the room. So like the parents of a child's imagination, they are indeed everywhere, even when not actually visible.

In part, therefore, the painting's abiding mystery is due to the ambiguity of subject matter, in much the same way as a dream's ambiguity relates to the distinction between its manifest and latent content. It appears to be about one thing (the infanta being painted in the splendour of the court, surrounded by her retinue) all of which are indeed there (the 'manifest' image) and superbly depicted, with the centrality of the princess holding our gaze. And at the same time, someone or something – the royal couple perhaps – invisible to the viewer, (but in the place where the viewer is standing) is holding *her* gaze. Is the child looking at her parents who have come into the room to inspect the portrait of their daughter, or has the daughter come into the room with her entourage to inspect a double portrait of her parents who are posing for the artist, the subjects of both the child's and the artist's concentration? Or has everyone come into the room, simply to watch the artist at work? Who is the subject and who is the object of the many gazes of the painting? We, the spectators, are increasingly bemused, our gaze captured and held in trying to work this out. Is it the princess? The maids? The royal couple? The court? Is it the invisible subject of the painting that can be seen only by the artist (but may be reflected in the mirror)?

The painter – off to the side and standing back – looks directly out at the viewer (or the invisible royal couple, or someone else entirely). Paintbrush in one hand, palette in the other, he stands – as if, at this very moment, interrupted – before the work on which he is currently engaged, whatever that may be. However, as the work on the easel takes up almost the entire space on the far left of the painting, thereby echoing both the edge, and the scale, of the painting actually before us, the suggestion is that the subject of the invisible painting whose back we can see is the one we are now viewing – this one. We are being teased into wondering if we would see this very painting, *'Las Meninas'*, if we could manage to peer round and glimpse the other side, the surface visible at present only to the artist, who may be tantalisingly offering the viewer an image of both the front and back of the work at the same time. Is he winking at us?

The setting for the painting is a large room in the palace (at the time, permanently designated as the artist's studio, but formerly the living room of the infanta's brother, the late, young Prince Balthasar) whose walls are hung with pictures. The collection, or parts of it, may have been either directly or indirectly influenced by Velasquez who was also appointed as the chief curator and adviser on acquisitions to the court, so the space in which the painting is set refers to both the king and the artist, who is here, literally and symbolically, 'in his element'. Although this might not have been understood by any outside the court, it would have been understood by both Velasquez and his patron.

This has some significance, for just as with prolonged analysis of a dream, answers become questions, give rise to associations and meaning continues to shift. We might say that the subject, or the equivalent of the 'dream-thought', in the painting is not the king, the queen, the infanta, the entourage or the grandeur of the court, but the creator of the image, the dreamer, for finally it is a self-portrait of the artist. In the stance described earlier, he is not 'interrupted' by unexpected visitors, but very much in the midst of working, looking at himself in a mirror in order to paint the portrait of himself that we see in the painting. And he is doing so, depicting himself at the heart of the most powerful kingdom of the time. It is his painting, his 'dream', and it is Velasquez who is putting everyone in his or her place, orchestrating the scene and the characters. What appears to be a celebration of the Spanish Court of Philip IV is, at the same time, a declaration of the artist's identity as master of his own realm. And the viewer is not, in *fact*, standing in the place where the king and queen might, by implication, be standing, but in the place of the artist. This is precisely where he stood to paint this picture, brush and palette to hand like symbols of state, mirror to one side and canvas before him. As with a dream, the subject is always the dreamer and amongst the many 'meanings' embedded in this painting, the 'wish' it expresses, or perhaps the question it poses, concerns 'who rules'?

This image, here shown as a small rectangle on a page in reproduction, can take up limitless space in writing and discourse – as this particular painting (but not only this painting) has in fact done. This would be true of many images, and not just a masterpiece such as this. And so it is with the dream – as Freud pointed out – and also, I suggest, the daydream. A picture is truly worth more than 1,000 words. (In fact, this one took 1,264 and has barely begun to scratch the surface).

The dream of Irma's Injection

These ideas can be further illustrated by once again turning to Freud's specimen dream, one with which readers may be familiar. I have summarised Freud's (1900) own summary, as follows:

> **"Specimen Dream"** (Dream of July 23rd–24th, 1895)
> *A large hall – numerous guests – Among them Irma whom Freud takes to one side, as though to reproach her for not having accepted his 'solution' [saying] 'If you still get pains, it's really only your fault.' Irma replies that her pains have now extended to her throat, stomach and abdomen, it's choking her. Freud is alarmed by this, and notes that she looks pale and puffy. He thinks to himself that he must have missed something, so takes her to the window to examine her throat. He notes, that 'she showed signs of recalcitrance, like women with artificial dentures', and thinks to himself that that was unnecessary. She then opens her mouth 'properly, and Freud notices a big white patch and other disturbing symptoms 'which were evidently modelled on the turbinal bones of the nose'. He calls in Dr. M., who looks different from usual, and who confirms Freud's findings. His friend Otto was now standing beside Irma, and another friend Leopold was percussing her through her bodice, where further symptoms are discovered. M. diagnoses an infection, but suggests that 'dysentery will supervene and the toxin will be eliminated.' Freud acknowledges that they know the source of the infection, which was most likely an injection Otto had given her of a preparation – the precise name of which momentarily escapes him, but comes to him in the image of the chemical formula, and he has the thought that 'probably the syringe had not been clean'.*

(107)

That summary can quite easily be imagined, brought to mind as a picture, as I have tried to show here (Figure 4.2). It is not too difficult to visualise a late 19th century Viennese 'salon'. We can picture Freud listening to Irma telling him of her complaint, inspecting her throat by the window. We follow the very graphic description of his examination, peering into her mouth, noting her symptoms, alongside further details of her physicality, her skin, her body and her dress. We can visualise his professional colleague's approach, one looking different from usual (perhaps representing more than one person) and the starkly visual image of the letters of the formula he sees 'written' before him. The manifest setting of the dream, the belle époque soirée, disguises the palpable discomfort inherent in the unfolding description, and eventual meaning of the dream. Freud's straightforward account of the imagery of the dream offers itself to the process of visual analysis in much the same way as one might approach the understanding of a painting not only on the basis of its content, but on its structure, composition,

Figure 4.2 Freud's 'Dream of Irma's Injection'.
Source: C. Carey.

tone, palette, configuration and juxtaposition of figures, its harmonies and disso-nances and so forth, that is to say, its 'style'.

Developments on representability

Repressed ideas may emerge in the form of images, as if trying to escape censor-ship by whatever means possible. An example would be Freud's repression of the name of the artist of the Orvieto fresco, Signorelli, in his illustration of for-getting as a commonplace defence, but having quite clearly in his mind an image of the artist's self-portrait within the fresco, which then did indeed fade as soon as he was eventually able to recall the name via a sequence of associations (1898:290–296), as well as to understand why it had been blocked in the first place. Thus, representability can be seen in terms of organising information such that it comes to consciousness along a continuum from perceptual, through image, to verbal – but may also retreat, if necessary, along the same path.

Horowitz (1972) comments that, with regard to image, 'skill at conceptual manipulation by formation of visual images is useful to architects, painters, sur-geons – and psychoanalysts during dream interpretation' (804). A further way of understanding the function of representability within psychoanalytic practice may be to recognise that visual images are effective for expressing and commu-nicating information about the form and spatial relationships of objects, which can then be understood in terms of feelings. As Freud (1900) demonstrated with dreams, and as we have seen with paintings, the plastic properties of imagery facilitate symbolisation, condensation and displacement often more effectively than words.

Staying with this aspect of dream-work, 'representability', the late James Fisher (2007), in an unpublished paper, indicates that Freud identifies this as the most critical element in understanding the dream. Fisher suggests that Bion's alpha-function can be seen as a development of Freud's theory of the dream-work com-ponent of representability (also described as 'figurability'[11]) or, what Fisher calls 'imaging'. He draws attention to the relationship between alpha-function and per-ception and the role of the sense impressions – those based on information, and those based on emotional experience – involved in that process. Fisher describes a session in which the therapist, responding to a disturbed child's manifest state of fear, enacted through evocative sounds – rather than words – something of his understanding of the child's projected, but otherwise incommunicable terror. He describes the clinical encounter as 'a spontaneous work of figurability', making the child's internal world more 'presentable', or capable of representation, when other forms of descriptive interpretation seemed unavailable including, in this particular case, the absence of imagery. The analyst, deprived of his customary tools of inter-pretation, felt 'menaced' by a nightmarish 'absence of any representation'. Fisher considers that the role of dream-work, specifically the process Freud described as the 'capacity for representation', equates with or with aspects of, both figuration and alpha-function (or reverie).

I suggest that this thinking can apply in a similar way to the daydream, in particular the therapist's daydream, in which case one understands the phenomenon not as a lapse in technique, but as an instinctive response to the need to understand, most commonly associated with maternal reverie. This draws attention to both the similarity and difference between uses and understandings of the terms 'daydream' and 'reverie'. In common parlance, they are more or less identical, but in clinical practice, the reverie, particularly as embraced by Bion, is generally if not universally, to be welcomed as a principle component of 'alpha-function', the processing of psychic chaos into psychic order, whereas the term 'daydream' may be more likely to be used to describe a distraction from the work in hand, a regrettable lapse (the possible motivations for which I discuss in Chapter 6). This distinction echoes to some extent that drawn between the positive, or useful, and negative or disrupting versions of countertransference described in the preceding chapter. However, if the dream-work, (or 'daydream-work') aspect of the daydream is accepted, and the daydream thereby becomes more amenable to interpretation, it takes on more of the favourable therapeutic characteristics of the maternal or clinical, 'reverie'.

Days' residues

Freud (1900) asserted that every dream bears some evidence of a link connecting it with the material of the previous day, that is, the usually incidental or seemingly negligible experience that enables an unconscious idea to gain entry into the quasi-conscious dream-space, as either idea, or image, or both; in this way, awkward but significant thoughts are smuggled in by donning the mottled camouflage of irrelevance. As he describes it, 'some recent impression … often of the most trivial kind' has been 'woven into' the 'texture' of the dream, since these have the 'least to fear from the censorship imposed by resistance' (563–564). He suggests that the reason for this is that as it is not possible for an unconscious idea to enter the preconscious on its own, it establishes a link with an idea that is already there and, in effect, slips or smuggles itself in undercover. I suggest, for the purposes of this discussion, that the day's residues are to the dream as the patient's presence or material is to the therapist's daydream.

Later, Freud (1913a) clarified some of these points further, stating that some of this material may represent unresolved wishes, fears, intentions, reflections, warnings, and so forth (273–274). This resonates with the concept of co-construction in the therapist's daydream, that is to say, if the patient's material particularly resonates with something unresolved in the therapist, both elements may contribute to the character of the daydream and the therapist would have to approach this in the same way she does countertransference material that overlaps with her own concerns and those of the patient.

Charles Fisher's extensive research on the subject of image construction in dreams (undertaken in the United States of America mainly during the 1950s) supports the relationship between the processes of representability to those of the 'days' residues'. He confirms well-documented early psychological experiments[12] (Fisher 1956, 1957) that suggest that subthreshold, or preconscious, visual perception influences dream imagery, and plays a role in transforming the dream-thoughts into visual images, commensurate with Freud's regard for plastic representability (Freud 1900:339–349). Fisher's research indicated that such perceptions find their way into the imagery of the mind in its waking state as well, and suggests a three-phase process of conscious perception consisting of first the registration of the percept; then the link with an earlier, similar memory or experience; and finally, the emergence into consciousness of the fresh percept (Fisher 1957:41–42). Olson (2000) comments that 'Fisher shows that perception takes place below the level of conscious awareness' and that 'percepts are subject to various transformations (multiplications, decompositions, fusions, fragmentations, displacements, distortions, and the like)' that 'begin immediately following perception. They resemble, and may be identical with, the operations of primary process described by Freud' (Olson 2000:385). He notes that Fisher's controlled research also suggests 'that dream-work begins during the day, at the time of perception' and 'occurs outside awareness' (ibid.:387). Olson also notes Fisher's corroboration of Freud's observation that unconscious ideas only enter consciousness under cover of a screen of similarity or association, emphasising the capacity of the day's residue to both evoke, and camouflage, unconscious fantasy.

Meltzer's dream-life

I conclude this section on the link between 'daydream-work' and daydream imagery, by considering Donald Meltzer's (1983) critical review of Freud's dream theory, with regard to the structure and function of the dream as a symbolic area of mental life, but from a Kleinian perspective, and with Bion's theory of thinking in mind. Meltzer takes issue with a number of Freud's assertions, such as the dream being the guardian of sleep, suggesting rather that the opposite may be true – that we sleep in order to dream (in fact, these may be mutually inclusive positions) – and critiques the function of the dream as wish-fulfilment, a term he finds ambiguous and unhelpful. I agree partly with Meltzer here in that regarding the dream so reductively as the expression of a wish, even when true, is neither all that it is, nor is it always clinically helpful. With regard to Freud's insistence concerning an infantile wish always being expressed in the dream, clinically I find it more helpful to understand the dream as *posing a question*, which may include a wish, or a need, to know, a wish to solve a riddle.

Meltzer specifically revisits Chapter VI of *The Interpretation of Dreams* (1900) and reconsiders the 'core' of the theory, the dream-work, whose processes are outlined above. In doing so, he aligns himself more closely with theories such as those of Ella Sharpe (1937), who draws attention to the dream's tendency to utilise linguistic and poetry-like characteristics such as simile, metaphor, alliteration, onomatopoeia and other literary aesthetic devices. Indeed, this is the heart of Meltzer's thesis, and is significant also in relation to my argument, which sees the analyst's visual reverie as functioning also within an aesthetic dimension: one that perceives or senses connectedness where it may not be obvious, recognising and intuitively responding to the similar in the dissimilar.

Meltzer sees it as the role of the analyst to listen, and help transform the dream description into meaning, by providing a process of symbolisation that will both order, and bestow order, on disjointed thoughts and feelings with patient and analyst together working out problems of symbolic representation at a non- or pre-verbal level. There is an understanding here that unconscious fantasy is a continuous process, in the background of conscious thought the whole time, and that dreaming is the unconscious fantasy that takes place during sleep, similar, by analogy, to the way in which a film that is being projected onto a screen in daylight only becomes visible in the dark. I would add to this that the daydreaming process of the therapist can be seen as the unconscious fantasy that takes place in the unique conditions and setting, or theatre, of the session.

Meltzer notes that, excepting Bion, the course of psychoanalysis has proceeded in a linguistic direction, but has taken less account of processes of, or disturbances in, thinking functions that have their origins in the pre-verbal stage (1983:66). Basing his reasoning on Bion's theories of thinking, whereby the emotional experience is prior to thought, and thought is prior to thinking, the dream – and I would include the daydream of the therapist – can be seen as performing a problem-solving function in pre-verbal terms, based fundamentally on the internalised dyadic relationship between mother and baby, with Bion's understanding of the mother's role as 'mind' providing the model for this function. This pre-verbal mode often takes the form of imagery, prior to being transformed into communicable language.

This construct provides a model of what might be described as a 'crucible' function of imagery within the reverie, which is similar to that performed by the mother who, while attempting to understand her baby's state of mind through observation, empathy, attunement, experience and reflection ('alpha-function'), is at the same time having to manage her own negative feelings of anxiety, uncertainty, self-doubt, anger, resentment and so forth.

Clinical example: Ms. G

An illustration of this function is taken from a session with a patient, Ms. G, who had difficulty in connecting experience with affect. She had been speaking for some sessions of a foreboding that seemed to have no foundation. During one session she had remembered, in passing, that the first occurrence of a particular symptom or tendency (a form of denial through intensely wished for magical reversal) took place when she was aged about six. She was with a group of grown-ups following the death of her paternal grandmother. She had little conscious memory of this grandmother, but distinctly remembers feeling her own distress at witnessing that of her father. She recalled that her overriding feeling

at the time – and one recurring regularly throughout her life in different circumstances – was a powerful wish to magically undo what had happened, to 'wind
back the clock'. She genuinely believed that she should be able to do this, to
restore order and tranquillity, and the frustration at not being able to do so was
almost unendurable.

In the session, she described the memory in a detached, self-deprecating way,
mocking her child-like grandiosity. My attention was partly on what the patient
was saying, partly on the detached way she was saying it, and partly, I eventually noticed, on an image that I began to realise had been at the back of my mind
for some time during this particular session, and very far removed, it seemed,
from the present material. The image was of a long, narrow, sun-filled playroom
in my grandfather's house that I regarded proprietorially as 'my own'. At one
end was a chest that contained the remnants of the toys of the children of the
family (my mother, aunts and uncles). This, for me, was a treasure chest since
these toys were nothing like my own, being of another era and, often, from
another country. They seemed to me utterly exotic. Favourite amongst these was
a cloth doll: it was a 'southern belle', with peachy complexion, blond curls, tiny
waist encircled by a long, tiered, flouncy skirt at the base of which there peeped
a white petticoat that, when you turned it over, became the practical gingham
checked skirt and white apron of the 'black mammy doll', on the other side. I
found this transformation fascinating, intrigued by the sudden reversal that, like
magic, came about by the mere flip of a simple piece of cloth. I would spend
ages doing this, flipping from the one to the other, trying to register the moment
of transition, as one doll magically transformed into another (although this also
meant that I was frustrated at not being able to play with both at the same time).

The memory of that room – always sunlit, and that doll – always alluring,
were similarly distracting on this occasion, although I was only vaguely aware
of it until I noticed the silence in the session, became conscious that my mind
had been elsewhere and reproached myself silently for my wandering attention.
However, I then noted the correspondence between Ms. G's mentioning the
death of her grandparent, and it struck me that the last time I actually visited that
once familiar space – or saw its contents – would probably have been just after
my own grandfather died. I remembered then that I too, like my patient, had
been mostly excluded from these events – the funeral and the mourning process
– that followed his death, which had had a profound effect on my mother, again
similar to Ms. G, disturbed by her parent's distress. The parallels then developed
further in that I was aware that although this was the first experience of death
that I had consciously encountered, sad as it was, it was not life-changing as was
the later death of a parent. I began to consider the possibility that the foreboding
my patient had been expressing was perhaps the fear of the death of her mother
(which was not imminent, but had been the subject of concern due to a recent
medical procedure), which was something that could not be thought about at all.
In reviewing this experience, it seems that as the patient was coming closer to
material that was potentially painful – in different ways, for both of us – I took

refuge in what first appeared to be a very pleasant memory, perhaps initially triggered by the mention of the age (six years) that Ms. G was at the time of her grandmother's death, and the age which I too was in the memory of playing with the doll. But the image also held references and associations to the more disturbing parallels of exclusion (from the grieving ritual and process), loss, the anxiety at seeing her father in this inconsolable state (the one she was now unconsciously anticipating for herself), and the retreat into denial through reversal, that I think were at the heart of the sense of detachment from feelings with which Ms. G was struggling. The fact that the fascinating doll also embodied a number of contradictions (including a form of 'reversal') – being both similar and different, visible and invisible and perhaps most significantly, separate and inseparable – may also have contributed to the relevance of the image for me in relation to my patient.

Put briefly, in the clinical situation, in moments of self-doubt, uncertainty, feeling distant or excluded from the patient's inner world, a space of reflection is necessary for the therapist to regain a sense of self-containment. Such a space is often provided by reverie, which may manifest itself in the form of a daydream activated, directly or indirectly, by the presence or material of the patient. The visual form of the daydream can provide a refuge from either confusion, precision of thought or, in more extreme circumstances, from something at present unthinkable. With anxiety reduced, a more relaxed, 'freely-floating', possibly more creative and playful state of mind emerges. In this state, the therapist is more open to associations, creating a bridge between her own and the patient's experience. In the illustration above, the idea of magical transformation (via reversal in the patient), and the magical transformation of the doll (from child to nanny-mother in the therapist) provided an affective associative link between the two participants that included the death of a grandparent, the distressing grief of a parent, the helplessness of the child to console, or to be consoled, as well as the memory of that first conscious brush – for both patient and therapist – with mortality.

Meltzer regarded dreaming as a form of unconscious thinking, similar to the role of play in infants and children, and the epistemological urge, or quest and discovery of meaning, in adults. This characteristic of the unconscious, he says:

> is strongly borne out in the consulting room by the phenomenon which some patients refer to as "flashes", sudden inexplicable, vivid visual images, seemingly unrelated to the immediate verbal exchange. When they are treated as dream images they yield a rich insight into the infantile transference active at the moment.
>
> (1983:89)

Meltzer states that the 'dreaming process has entered the conversation' and 'entered as a visual language ... worth a thousand words', (ibid.) thus, viewing dreams and I would add, daydreams or visual reverie, as a form of internal language, whose vocabulary, grammar, syntax and structure can be usefully learned and understood. This would apply similarly to both patient and therapist.

Meltzer also considers the relationship between 'dream-space' and 'mental-space' as distinct, but overlapping internal geographies, whose form and complexity may indicate the dimensionality of the internal world. This has significance with regard to the suggestion that the nature of the therapist's daydream has relevance concerning the characteristics of the patient's internal world. The roots of language are primitive and this has a bearing on the way in which thoughts occur in more regressive states, suggesting that it is possible to surmise the internal state of the patient by the quality or style of his language, and – I argue – his imagery, alongside that which arises in the therapist in the presence of the patient.

Summary

In considering 'representability', or modes and processes of visualisation and image construction in the dream, and aligning these with the daydream, it is possible to see that many of the processes of the dream-work as originally described by Freud, and since elaborated upon by others, have a counterpart in the daydream of the therapist. A similar 'deconstruction' of the daydream may yield useful associations to the therapist's responses to the patient, just as might be done with interpreting a dream. Further, these processes, at least in part, serve the similar dual function of both locking and unlocking the psyche, whether defensively or expressively, which is the subject of the next chapter.

Notes

1   Another observation, which is constantly repeated, relates to the patient's spontaneous reproductions. It may be asserted that every single reminiscence, which emerges during an analysis of this kind has significance. An intrusion of irrelevant mnemic images (which happen in some way or other to be associated with the important ones) in fact never occurs. An exception which does not contradict this rule may be postulated for memories, which unimportant in themselves, are nevertheless, indispensable as a bridge, in the sense that the association between two important memories can only be made through them.

2 In *Studies on Hysteria* (1893) Freud describes the process with Fräulein Elisabeth von R.: 'It was as though she were reading a lengthy book of pictures, whose pages were being turned before her eyes' (153).

3 Silberer, H. (1909) 'Bericht über eine Methode, gewisse symbolische Halluzinations-Erscheinungen hervorzurufen und zu beo-bachten', *Jb. psychoanal. psychopath. Forsch., 1,* 513. (49, n. 2, 102, n. 1, 344–345, 378, 412, n. 503–505).

4 Herbert M. Wyman and Stephen M. Rittenberg, in the 'editors' introduction to Volume 1, no. 2' of the *Journal of Clinical Psychoanalysis* (International Universities Press, Inc., 1992). This collection of papers by Otto Isakower on the 'analyzing instrument' were not published at the time they were written, but held in the records of the meetings of the New York Psychoanalytic Institute where Dr. Isakower was Chairman of the Curriculum Committee, and gathered together for publication in 1992.

5 In *Screen Memories* (1899) Freud showed that what appeared to be isolated, but vivid, images drawn from early experience were in fact partial constructions and synthetisations, combinations of fact, defence, wish and denial, sustained via repression and displacement as a safer, more manageable version of a disturbing memory or event.

6 The underlying, latent, often difficult, idea with which the dreamer is wrestling, that is expressed symbolically through the content of the dream.

7 'The notion of après-coup is important for the psychoanalytical conception of temporality. It establishes a complex and reciprocal relationship between a significant event and its resignification in afterwardness, whereby the event acquires new psychic efficiency' (from Laplanche, J. 2002, Après-coup. In: de Mijolla A, editor. *Dictionnaire international de la psychanalyse*. Paris: Calmann-Levy. 121).

8 As set out in, for example, *Course in General Linguistics*, trans. Wade Baskin, Glasgow, Fontana/Collins, 1974.

9 G.T. Fechner in a passage from his 'Elemente der Psychophysik' in Liébeault, A.A. *Le sommeil provoqué et les états analogues*, Paris, (1889, 2:520–521).

10 As Breuer comments. 'The mirror of a reflecting telescope cannot at the same time be a photographic plate.' Breuer and Freud, 1895, *fn.*

11 Term used by C. and S. Botella (2005:31–34).

12 Otto Poetzl (1926) carried out experiments on dream formation following tachistoscopic (very brief, i.e. 1/100 second) exposure of pictures to subjects, which although not consciously perceived, nonetheless, appear in the manifest content of subsequent dreams. (Poetzl, O. (1917). Experimentall erregte Traumbilder in ihren Beziehungen zum indirekten Sehen Ztsch. *Neurol. & Psychiat. 37*:278–349).

Chapter 5

Dynamics of imagery

Visual memory-images are of course more difficult to disavow than the memory-traces of mere trains of thought.

(Freud 1895b:299)

Defensive and progressive strategies

In this chapter I want to discuss further how ideas of 'representability' work in the clinical setting. As noted previously, visualisation is a dynamic process that can function both defensively as well as threateningly: defensively, in the sense of providing a refuge from, or avoidance of, more explicit articulation through language; and threateningly in that, being a more primal, regressive form of ideation, can unwittingly give rise to mental imagery that then itself fosters anxious associations. This results in a tendency towards oscillation between the two modes of ideation, linguistic and visual.

But further and perhaps from a more creative perspective clinically, the capacity for visualisation may also function as a type of 'crucible', a temporary retreat offering a reflective space of containment where difficult, complex or indigestible thoughts may be processed and absorbed gradually. This iterative process allows for the valuable clinical tool of fresh insight.

It seems that we may seek refuge from uncomfortable thoughts by escaping into imagery, but may also find that the more relaxed 'border conditions' of that retreat can equally allow in just those unwanted intrusive associations we were attempting to escape in the first place. With that in mind, I suggest that image and thought tend to hold each other in a form of defensive-creative balance or tension, with one providing a potential refuge from the other when either threatens impingement.

Primary process

Horowitz (1970) reminds us that Freud (1900) noted the central use of visual images in primary process thinking in the formation of dream pictures, and adds that this characteristic mechanism of primary process 'is achieved when thought is expressed through the visual image', that is to say, not *only* in dreams. In describing modes of representation of thought, he remarks on the close relationship of images to emotional processes with regard to recollection. And, of particular significance here, Horowitz writes:

> in the course of psychoanalytic psychotherapy ... painful and repressed memories and impulses may enter awareness *first as images* [my emphasis] – either in fantasy, free association, or dream – and only later be labelled with words.... Images (as thoughts in general) may be formed in response to emotions; images may express emotions; and images may evoke emotions.
>
> (73–74)

And, further, that while not exclusive to primary process thinking, 'in psychoanalytic theory, visual images are often tacitly considered to be the characteristic mode representing primary process type thoughts' (ibid.). He continues that images may enter awareness 'in a spontaneous flow that seems mysteriously unguided by intention', and it is likely that censorship is less active over image formation than words, a feature exploited by analysts (Freud 1895b; Jung 1959; Kubie 1943; Ferenczi 1950, inter alia) who all encouraged their patients to think in visual images rather than in words – where such images relating to repressed material did not occur spontaneously – in order to subvert the defensive processes in play. Just as Horowitz considers that this model enables a more dimensional understanding of the patient's character, inner world, object relationships, as well as levels of regression and defence, the therapist may equally fruitfully apply this technique to herself.

Dual function of imagery

In considering the uses to which imagery is put in the clinical setting, it is helpful to begin with Freud's (1900) suggestion that reversion to imagery may be a defensive response to 'involuntary ideas' emerging, provoking a 'change into visual and acoustic images' (102)[1] that, according to Mark Kanzer (1958) normally, 'dissipate the disturbing idea in the very process of perception; a solution which ... is fundamental for dream and for æsthetic enjoyment as well as for free association' (465). As in the 'fort-da' example, the baby's game indicates that there is a progressive development from this form of image-for-object substitution towards increasing abstraction, and eventual verbalisation and abstract conceptualisation, no longer reliant on gesture or picture to communicate (although these may still be vestigial, unconsciously present, and expressed in posture, facial expression, involuntary gesture, stance, tone, dream, daydream and so forth).

However, I now want to develop this idea of image as refuge, as I indicated earlier. Although it appears that we retreat defensively away from verbal articulation *towards* the image, it is equally – or at least also – possible that, just as defensively, we turn away from the image, at times employing a form of scot-omisation.[2] To some extent, and as with a dream, this may depend upon the dual capacity of the dream or daydream camouflage simultaneously to conceal as well as to reveal the unwanted thought – as a camouflage webbing or fabric may conceal the surface or the detail, but not the form or shape, of an object, such as a weapon, for example. A further approach to imagery and visualisation, however, suggests an alternative dynamic, one that follows the to-and-fro move-ment of retreat and re-engagement.

Oscillation

René Spitz (1956), for example, in a paper on the shifting role of countertrans-ference, follows Ernst Kris's (1950, 1953) ideas with regard to regression in the service of the ego to understand the process by which the analyst comprehends his patient beyond intellectual understanding. He conveys that the detachment and objectivity that is part of empathic identification can be equated with this form of regression as it manifests itself in individuals (e.g. visual artists and poets) who appear to have greater access to regressive material while at the same time being able to transform it into a secondary process elaboration. While accepting that some practitioners may indeed have more ready access to their dreams or to their regressive fantasies or non-verbal (self) communication than others, this reversibility of regression that remains under the control of the auto-nomous, less conflict-driven, ego is well recognised as a useful tool of the ana-lytic process. This suggests that although visualisation within a daydream or reverie may take one of a number of forms, in each case – whether defensive retreat from, or a regressive (but non-defensive) embrace of imagery – it serves a dynamic function for both the therapist and the therapy.

Defensive flights into imagery (from secondary to primary process)

In the late 1950s and early 1960s, two significant papers exploring image forma-tion appeared, the first in 1958 (already briefly referred to above) by Mark Kanzer and the second, in 1961, by Max Warren. In the first one, Kanzer understands free association (a regressive process) as an oscillation between image and idea whereby, on the one hand – as described above on image formation in the hypna-gogic state – relaxation of secondary process encourages visualisation, while ver-balising 'whatever comes to mind' prioritises abstract articulation over image. He observes that a disturbance in free association forces the patient to find a com-promise through a form of 'verbal imagery', similar to the visual quality of the dream (465). This regressive transformation from thought/word to image (or other non-verbal form of expression) helps to reduce anxiety. According to Kanzer, the analyst's attention to such imagery fosters insight into the patient's psychic pro-cesses, as they take refuge in different levels of consciousness in an effort to escape scrutiny. This may be evident, for example, when a patient breaks off from narrative speech, with the sudden memory of a dream or other visual idea that may be understood as indicative of such a shift. Kanzer cites Deutsch (1953) who saw imagery in analysis as a form of both resistance *and* communication, and Lewin (1955) who regarded deviations from verbalisation and retreat into imagery as a flight from secondary process functioning. However, Kanzer nonetheless, sees the interplay between imagery and ideation, between primary and secondary process, as also a normal oscillation.[3] Kanzer, Deutsch and Lewin were describing defensive flights into imagery in relation to the patient, but they would apply equally to the defensive processes of the therapist.

Horowitz (1970), too, comments on the developmental progression from image to word, but notes that little attention has been paid to the phases of image thinking, there being a further supposition that this process in adults is predominantly lexical, based on the assumption of the primacy of words. However, researchers such as Humphrey (1951) conclude that 'while thinking is permeated with language, it is not identical with word usage', and proposed that images may also be used defensively to distract from thinking (or, conversely, they might enhance thinking by associative enrichment). He describes a gradual progression from imaging, then intellectualising the image and then relinquishing the image in favour of symbols, towards imageless knowledge or abstraction. This progression, I think, accurately and inevitably, describes much psychoanalytic discourse.

Not in terms of defence, but more neutrally, Horowitz also cites research by Paivio (1969), suggesting that memory utilises two processes: one based on images in relation to spatial representations, and the other on words, in relation to sequential processing. These two modes would also represent a more 'neutral', rather than an emotional (or defensive), understanding of the oscillation between word and image that the therapist characteristically experiences within the session.

Kanzer speaks too of the tendency to prioritise the auditory over the visual, and the concept over the image. However, these subordinated modes become lodged in the preconscious where they can be accessed and brought forward when resistance impedes the otherwise more favoured language.

> The emphasis on verbalization during free association also obscures the relation of image to idea. Progress in treatment may actually be marked by the interruption of free association and the emergence of the background imagery, rather than words, as resistance diminishes and true relaxation occurs.
>
> (481–482)

Again, such a case would clearly not represent a defence, but a capacity to harness and make use of primary process, much as Ernst Kris (1953) describes within the creative process and, once again, the principle would apply to both participants.

Kanzer describes the sometimes subtle fluctuation within the psychoanalytic session between levels of consciousness, and how these may be detected through attending to the variation in use of idiom employed by the patient, from full consciousness to deep regression. Citing Freud (1900:14), Kanzer reinforces the idea that resistance to unwanted thoughts prevents such disturbing ideas from becoming conscious, but rather transforms them into perceptual components, such as visual and auditory images, similar to the visual images of the dream. This would apply to metaphoric figures of speech, the use of figurative language, references to physical surroundings, colour, sound and so forth. In other words, use of imagery can be understood as a form of resistance, a subterfuge or camouflage, but may also be seen as a cipher, which when 'decoded', reveals the very thoughts and messages that are seeking refuge. Once again, this observation may be applied equally to both parties. It is particularly evocative of the apparently 'wandering' type of daydream, that appears, often deceptively, as a 'non-sequitur' in relation to the ongoing session, but that may prove relevant both in terms of harbouring clues to understanding material that remains unarticulated, or not yet articulable, through language. The mental picture of the cityscape in the previous chapter (p. 63) is an example of such a seemingly unrelated image whose persistence and repetition provoked the enquiry into its potential significance.

Horowitz (1970) also notes the defensive function embodied in shifts in the mode of experience from words to images, suggesting that conversion from lexical thought or speech to image formation may act as a form of resistance, momentarily distancing the patient from contact with the analyst, the patient being able to keep the image to himself more easily than he would verbalised thoughts, which he may feel pressed to voice. I would add that, at the same time, it is also the case that visual images afford an immediate depiction of the relationships of objects due to the simultaneous organisation of information in a single image, which – particularly with repetition – may be indicative of aspects of the nature of such relationships or that may suggest fluctuating developmental positions. Thus, once imagery makes itself conscious, it begins to provide a more representational function insofar as images – in both dreams and daydreams – incorporate formal details of relationships of objects, texture, form, tone, contrast, harmony, movement, rhythm, pace, space and so forth, that shed light on affective experience, whether the patient's or therapist's. This point is also made by Horowitz who speaks about the representational capacity of visual images, through the juxtaposition of form, structure and spatial relationships of objects, to depict or suggest the nature and degree of feeling, particularly where such states evade verbal articulation. If, at this stage, the image can be elicited from the patient or brought to consciousness by the therapist, it may be treated as would a dream image within the session. This process is amply illustrated by Freud's numerous instances of image and word-play, notably the well-known 'aliquis' example he provides in *The Psychopathology of Everyday Life* (1901:9–14), in which the image of a saintly relic provides the associative clues to the forgetting by repression of a word, relating to an area of psychic discomfort that his companion, in the anecdote, wished to avoid.[4] This is also somewhat similar to the earlier example here, (p. 70) in which my patient dreams of herself in a purple dress, an image that reveals the wish, when verbalised during the ensuing conversation, to be 'inviolate'.

Ambiguity

Both the dream-work, and what I have called 'daydream-work' processes described earlier (that include condensation, displacement and overdetermination) are all marked by a complexity or ambiguity, that is the result of the many possible associations that any one image may provoke (such as the painting described earlier, open to multiple interpretations, all of which have contextual validity). This ambiguity may be defensively exploited in that it makes available numerous sources of association, in a manner similar to that delineated by Freud with regard to image construction in the dream, where he points out that the dream profits from the disguise afforded by imagery, since it may both reveal and conceal that which is pressing towards, while at the same time taking flight from, expression.

> If one ambiguous word is used instead of two unambiguous ones the result is misleading; and if our everyday, sober method of expression is replaced by a pictorial one, our understanding is brought to a halt, particularly since a dream never tells us whether its elements are to be interpreted literally or in a figurative sense or whether they are to be connected with the material of the dream-thoughts directly or through the intermediary of some interpolated phraseology.
>
> (Freud 1900:341)

Clearly, such ambiguity may be exploited by the patient's or the therapist's retreat into imagery or daydream, when either seeks to avoid something more explicit that may be uncomfortable.

Image as source of gratification

Horowitz also makes reference to the gratification or reassurance to be had through image formation, much as with the infant's hallucination of the breast or daydreams of rewarding moments, which as we have seen, tend to arise under conditions of anxiety, frustration, irritation or dissatisfaction to provide a form of visual compensation. This 'strategy' would extend to the therapist, as well, in terms of taking refuge in images of having or achieving, what may in the moment feel absent, elusive, unachievable or lost. This is closer to the commonplace understanding of the term 'daydreaming' as a form of wishful thinking, as in, 'Wouldn't it be nice …?'

Defence against imaging and imaging as defence

On the basis of research conducted by both himself and others (Foulkes and Fleisher 1975; Foulkes, Spear, and Symonds, 1966; Vogel, Foulkes, and Trossman, 1966), Suler (1989) considers the possible factors contributing to 'low and high imagery ability'. There is some evidence to support the thesis that 'poor imagers may be blocked from unconscious ideation by rigid defenses, whereas fluent, vivid imagers may be more adept at exploring unconscious processes and tapping warded-off affect' with also greater fluency of free association, and some implications for 'greater cognitive flexibility' (355). However, it was also shown that 'patients who dwell on their imagery may be resisting the analytic process or attempting to escape contact with the analyst' an observation that could apply equally to the therapist. Suler continues:

> Excessively intense and uncontrolled imagery – hallucinations being the most extreme example – may indicate ego defect or immaturity. The ability to control and objectively evaluate imagery may be a more important variable revealing psychopathological level than simply the clarity of the image. Imagery vividness, affective intensity, and controllability can be conceptualized as continua, with both the low and high poles associated with psychopathology.

> (355)

I now go on to discuss this counterpart to the defensive use of imagery, that is, the equally defensive flight *from* imagery.

Anxious imagery (flights from imagery to verbalisation: from primary to secondary process)

Just as the use, or avoidance, of imagery may indicate distinctive mental positions or shifts therein, so we may also observe similar strategies with the use or avoidance of language. Flights to imagery from language and flights to language from imagery, may both be understood as defences where visualisation in the first instance, or verbalisation in the second, provide retreats from anxious or depressive states that arise from over-articulation, whether verbal or visual.

In the second of the two papers on image formation referred to earlier, (and also here in Chapter 4 pp. 58–59) Max Warren (1961) draws attention, this time, to *avoidance* of image formation, and illustrates how verbalisation can function in the service of resistance within a conflictual state. He reasons, however, that psychic conflict provokes a regression similar to that of dream formation in which ideas are transformed cryptically into visual images, less open to communication, but – when attention is drawn to their presence – also more difficult to deny, due to the capacity for persistence of imagery. In the earlier chapter, I included his example of a patient who, during a lapse in speech, is invited to describe what he 'saw' (rather as Freud did in the early days), and he immediately responded with a description of the prehistoric animal devouring a man from which other associations rapidly flowed. On that occasion the significance of the pauses could be seen as a defensive silence during the shifting of scenes and levels, warding off awareness of oral instinctual impulses in relation to the transference. At first, verbalisation was avoided or unavailable, creating a blank space, a pause; when prompted, however, the patient could describe what appeared to be an innocuous, unrelated image; then, following his associations, he was able to gather words and images together to more ably approach the uncomfortable thought that was seeking refuge from explicit articulation, whether verbal or visual. The less threatening image allowed an opening to both admitting, as well as expressing, a difficult thought.

If the analyst becomes sensitive to such lapses in his patient's associations, and is able to elicit the underlying imagery, then the patient becomes sensitised to both the existence and the value of such imagery and may learn to retrieve it spontaneously when it may be treated as 'any psychic manifestation', by-passing the patient's effort to 'keep the analyst "out of the picture"' (508). That is to say, treating even such elusive images as any other association, more readily enables interpretation of the defence. I am suggesting that these same observations may be applied to the therapist's visual imagery, first in terms of noticing the image, which may appear vague, unrelated or inconsequential, then in noting its persistence, and ultimately – once it has been 'noticed'– treating it as 'any psychic manifestation'. For the therapist, this would mean developing a process for noticing and 'scanning' images for potential associations and possible usefulness.

However, getting hold of the image, once it has become conscious, may also be problematic since, as Freud (1893) observed, once a picture has emerged from the patient's memory, it is often the case that it then begins to fragment and dissipate as he attempts to describe it, as if the image is dissolved by words (as so often happens with dream imagery). He says, the 'picture becomes fragmentary and obscure in proportion as he proceeds with his description of it. *The patient is, as it were, getting rid of it by turning it into words* [author emphasis] ...' (280). Freud returns to this theme in *The Ego and the Id* (1923), where he restates the need to bear in mind 'the importance of optical memory residues – those of things (as opposed to words)' and to remember that 'it is possible for thought-processes to become conscious through a reversion to visual residues, and that in many people this seems to be the favoured method' (Freud 1923:21).[5] This would also suggest that there is an optimal moment for the grasping of imagery as a clinical tool, and it includes not only the moment of becoming aware of the image, but also acknowledging its characteristic elusiveness.

Continuing with anxiety around imagery, Lewin (1968) also speaks of fear, in some, of the power of the image to arouse 'ghosts', frightening ideas or unwanted memories. However, he suggests, that whatever has been taken in, in pictorial form, is potentially capable of being recollected and further, echoing

Freud, that 'early images persist, even though they may fall into disuse, or may be repressed' and may be held palimpsest-like in storage, living in composite proximity, again reminiscent of Freud's phantom Rome (Freud 1930:69–70), 'the four-dimensional picture of the different Romes, from the earliest city square to the present day, all standing in the same space' (as cited in Lewin 1968:64). Or we could equally think of Italo Calvino's repeated iteration of Venice in *Invisible Cities* (1974 [1972]) in which not only is a single linear narrative inadequate to describe the place, but so much so that each description requires endowing the same place with a different name.

The 'ghost' reference is also reminiscent of the dynamic repression described in *The Uncanny* (Freud 1919), where Freud says that whenever emotional impulses are repressed, they are transformed into anxiety (240–243). The uncanny object is most often an embodied object, a fearsome image or sound, and its appearance, being feared, is something to be discouraged or avoided, as would images (for example, within the session) that may be associated with the original anxiety or trauma.

Lewin indicates a further dynamic between speech and imagery where he speaks of the predominantly visual thinking of childhood as the 'pictorial past', and the tendency for this mode of thought to yield in time to verbalisation, as imageless thinking is seen as more abstract, sophisticated and mature. He concurs with Abraham (1913) that the universal tendency to visualisation may be inhibited, inter alia, by anxiety related to scopophilia, but that unconscious or preconscious imaging may conversely be a return to this need or wish, to see: the infant into the mind of the parent; the patient into the mind of the analyst; and certainly, the analyst into the mind of the patient. The analyst's scopophilic instinct is thus, aroused, thereby also arousing his anxiety and inhibition.

In relation to the scopophilic instinct, Lewin suggests that with some analysts, images come unbidden while listening to the patient. He writes:

> The analyst's sublimated scopophilia ... is not so much a matter of conscious imagery as it is of a certain visual undertone beneath his consciousness as he attends to analytic material. His consciousness may include visual images or may be imageless ... (producing) subtonic visual constructions, either with contents familiar to the analyst because of his self-study, training, and experience; or they may be "discoveries". As vicarious memories for his analysand (or for himself), scenes are the analytic products best suited for independent verification.
>
> (Lewin 1968:19)

Scotomisation

In his writing on both inhibitions (1926) and fetishism (1927), Freud also spoke of the phenomenon of scotomosation,[6] a form of repression or denial, a defence against threatening perceptions or resistance to seeing something unacceptable.

A couple of incidental examples from the perspective of the patient illustrate how commonplace this can be. Not many weeks after a patient started in therapy at three times a week, she came with a dream that involved arriving at my house and, instead of coming into the consulting room, went past the door and directly up the stairs, before coming back down for her session. She commented: 'The dream seemed very real, the house was just as it is, and the consulting room was just where it is, although I don't know where the staircase is here.' I was somewhat surprised by this statement as, although the patient would never have used it, the staircase is easily visible as you approach the consulting room from the entrance hall. It is impossible not to see it. Although she could not consciously recognise or acknowledge her curiosity about what happened 'upstairs', to the point of not allowing herself to notice what was directly in front of her, her unconscious had registered exactly where the stairs were, as represented in the dream.

A similar example comes from a patient who, after having been coming to sessions for some months, walked in and asked with some surprise, 'Has that tree always been there? I've never seen it before.' The tree, which is quite large and once again impossible not to notice when approaching the front door has been there for many years. There was nothing different about it between one day and the next, and yet it seems that this was the first time the patient was able to 'see' it. You cannot see what you don't see, so I imagine that similar 'blind spots' occur with the therapist as well, which unless they are somehow brought to her attention, may remain invisible. Classically, we may think of Oedipus blinding himself in horror at the crimes he had 'blindly' committed, a refusal to see something that should have been apparent. In Freud's theory of fetishism, the denial is initially visual, the refusal to acknowledge the absence of the penis in the mother, provoking the need to find or invent a replacement object or fetish, as a substitute for the one that is missing, lost or punitively destroyed. Socially, forms of visual denial, scotomisation, are commonplace in everyday life, in uncomfortable situations to which we unconsciously turn a 'blind eye'.

Further dynamic functions of imagery

I have already referred to the role of the defences of distortion generally, and displacement specifically, in the section on dream-work. Insofar as we may regard aspects of the dream-work as a defensive process, we may also consider the role that other strategies may play in the therapist's self-protective armour, and how they may manifest themselves in the imagery of the daydream. Such processes may include denial and reaction formation (for example, when confronting feelings of ignorance, incompetence or other experiences of inadequacy); projection (of unwanted feelings into or beyond, the patient); dissociation (such as taking temporary flight into an alternative or idealised self-identity); identification with the aggressor; grandiosity (for example, wish-fulfilling daydreams conjuring images of success and achievement or deflecting failure or frustration); intellectualisation (to avoid emotional anxiety); repression (ignorance, naiveté or forgetting), and such imagery as may indicate sublimation, or self-idealisation. Any, or any combination, of these defences may emerge in the imagery that comes into the therapist's mind during a session, often seemingly incidental, just on the edge of awareness, apparently disconnected from the patient or his material.

In an unusual paper on the self-analysis of the countertransference, Ross and Kapp (1962) explored the therapist's use of his or her visual images that arose in response to the patient's dreams. Stimulated by a talk given by Kanzer on image formation during free association, (see p. 86, Kanzer 1958) the authors here endeavour to formulate a technique for analysing the therapist's unconscious reactions to the patient or his transference (644). The method consists of using the analyst's associations to his or her visual images of the patient's dreams, a technique that appears to provide 'a simple spontaneous starting point which can be applied either when a countertransference problem has already been suspected or, routinely, to test for countertransference, even without other clues' that 'led the authors to pay attention to the visual images which came to mind while listening with "evenly suspended attention" as patients told their dreams' (645).

An example from their research touches on some of the defensive positions. The patient reports a disturbing dream that concerns a friend, also in analysis, who shared her house, but who came to say that she would be moving away. On hearing the dream, the therapist visualises a detail of the setting, encapsulated in a single word, '*dinette*'. This prompts a succession of associations from his own experience (no longer apparently related directly to the patient or her dream), that are linked in his mind initially to a flirtatious, superficial, boring, demanding colleague and then to a similarly emotionally demonstrative and demanding housekeeper from his childhood, whose eventual – although premature – departure came as a relief. At this point, the analyst considered the possibility that he had been subtly and unconsciously discouraging the erotic transference in his patient by encouraging her – again, subtly and unconsciously – to leave, a feeling that seems to have been picked up, and expressed, in the patient's dream. It was not, however, the dream *narrative* that at first communicated the transference and countertransference position, but a visual detail of the *setting* (the room in which the dream encounter was enacted) an otherwise neutral, apparently innocuous, detail. It was the therapist's imagistic association to the patient's dream-space that enabled the difficult feeling he had in relation to the patient to be revealed to his conscious awareness, and then recognised as having significance. Through inward reflection, the therapist was able to acknowledge to himself that recent interpretations prior to the dream had been defensively 'colored by unconscious feelings of wanting to reject the patient' and 'presented in a manner which contributed to the patient feeling that she was being criticized and excluded by her therapist' (Ross and Kapp 1962:647–648).

A second example from the same source has a similar point of departure – that is, a patient's dream setting, that leads to a more self-idealised set of associations. Several dreams took place in the back yard and driveway of the patient's early adolescent home, a setting that provoked the analyst's visualisation of a recent home of his own where he 'saw' his young son playing, as well as an earlier childhood home, which he associated with a toy car that had been bought for him, but then taken away, by his father who decided he was not yet big enough to operate it. These associations drew the analyst's attention to his tendency to equate the patient with both his own young son, as well as with his own adolescent, oedipal self and a recognition of the unconscious competition taking place within himself in relation to the patient's father. This awareness led the analyst to reviewing assumptions about the patient's father that the analyst was now able to see more clearly as projections, in which he had unwittingly participated (Ross and Kapp 1962:648–649).

Screen memory

Another illustration of a defensive, but potentially revealing, image is found in the phenomenon of 'screen memories' (Freud 1899), already referred to briefly, that may be seen as an inversion of the ambiguity of imagery, in that the vividness or reliable persistence of even an uncomfortable image or scene may be used as a form of visual decoy to block or disguise an even more uncomfortable memory or idea. To some extent, the example in the previous chapter illustrating *overdetermination* (in which the therapist's image of the 'conference' unfolds into a reminiscence about the inaccessible father) can be seen, initially, as a screen memory, insofar as it referred to a memorable and vivid, but seemingly innocuous image with personal associations, which at the same time concealed the more disturbed memories that created a bridge linking to the patient's own emotional landscape (p. 66). With regard to defensive processes, it is once again clear that the ambiguous nature of the image is both expedient and exploitable, as described earlier, in relation to dream (and daydream) imagery.

From the forgoing discussion on the continuous oscillation between imagery and verbalisation, we can see that while imaging and visualisation can be understood as a refuge from explicit, articulated speech, it is also the case that speech and verbalisation can be seen as a refuge from more primitive, anxious states that may be aroused by imagery.

Clinical example: Mrs. H

A simple illustration comes from a patient, Mrs. H, who had spoken from time to time of a vivid memory of being taught to swim at around the age of four or five by her father during a summer vacation that was shared with other families. The memory is mainly warm and pleasurable, but always includes a persistent note of anxiety that has to do with a worry that her father might think she was ready to swim before she was able, would let go of her and she would drown. Mrs. H recalled having a similar anxiety when first learning to ride a bike, a year or two later, and worrying that her father would think she could balance before she really was able to do so, meaning that he would let go prematurely and she would fall. Both these memories seemed at first to do with the pleasure of being the focus of her father's attention as well as an accompanying anxiety that had to do with being either too 'advanced', so father would think she no longer needed him, or not advanced enough, in which case the fear was that he would lose interest in her.

On one occasion, however, while describing the beach memory in some detail, including delighting in her new swimming costume and being excited by the novelty swimming aids her father had bought her, Mrs. H stopped speaking and said, 'I feel suddenly warm, as if I'm blushing.' She went on:

> I don't know why that should be, because all that I've just remembered is that one morning that summer when my father was teaching me to swim, one of the family friends that was holidaying with us brought their little girl to the beach. She was a little younger than me, and very sweet. My father was supporting me with one hand under my back in the water, when he called to the little girl, saying that she could come along too and learn to swim, and reached out his other hand to her. I think that that was when I thought I was going to drown. It wasn't just a worry that he would not be concentrating enough on me, it was a worry that I had, or might, become invisible to him – that I no longer existed.

After a pause, she added, 'I think that might have been the first time that I remember being aware of the feeling of jealousy, or possessiveness.'

She remembered the shock of this feeling as something almost annihilating. She wanted to protest that this was *her* father, not the other child's, 'and he wasn't allowed to teach anyone to swim but me'. She felt he could not have known what he was doing, since to do so would be, in the patient's eyes, tantamount to replacing her with the other little girl. The experience, at the time, left her feeling disorientated and confused. The development of the associations linked to this memory that came to her during this particular session provided the first conscious awareness she seems to have had concerning the actual emotional impact of that incident, which had until then, always been concealed by the more pleasurable memory. The element of anxiety had always been there, but falsely attributed to both her fear of the water as well as to the worry of disappointing her father or, alternatively, losing his attention. The anxiety she felt was therefore, held in the tension between seeming to be either too 'babyish' or too 'grown-up' for her father's undivided attention (and, intriguingly, both examples have to do with learning to find one's 'balance'). The emotional importance had been hidden behind the 'screen' of the sunny summer when her father had taught her to swim, not the sunny summer when she first felt the shocking stab of jealousy.

As a screen memory, this image functions in a number of ways. In the first instance, the recollection itself was mainly pleasurable, and linked to further memories of herself and her father, often as an exclusive pair. It was the strange persistence of the image that arose at various times during the sessions that led to both the patient and the therapist wondering about its regular inclusion in her thoughts and, from there, gradually to the association with the more painful feelings that had not been previously, consciously, linked to the image. Further, it gradually became clear that this incident would not in fact have been the first time that the patient had actually felt jealousy, but the earlier occasions were (so far) consigned to infantile amnesia. Now it became clear that this was a feeling that was so difficult to assimilate that it had been hitherto assiduously disavowed in her life, very notably absent in the content of the sessions hitherto, masked by her more conscious preoccupation with precociousness, pressure to perform and fear of failure.

Summary

In thinking about the dynamics of imagery, I describe how visualisation in the clinical setting is neither passive nor incidental, but can be a dynamic and at times a strategic process. Recourse to visualisation may be a defence against the clarity of verbal articulation, but conversely, finding refuge in speech may be a flight from the associative power of imagery and has its roots in primary process functioning. Research in this field suggests that this process is linked to conditions that foster regression, and occur more readily in hypnagogic states. I discuss some of the characteristics that are associated with image formation such as oscillation, ambiguity, scotomisation and screen memory. These processes impact similarly on both patient and therapist, and are often manifest in the therapist's daydream, that I now go on to discuss in greater detail.

Notes

1 Kanzer quotes an alternative version of this statement as it appears in *The Interpretation of Dreams* New York: The Modern Library, 1950, as follows: 'Emerging undesired ideas are changed into visual and auditory images' (14).

2 Freud (1926) employs the term following Laforgue (1926) and goes on to discuss it at greater length the following year in his paper on 'Fetishism' (1927).

3 Referring to 'A Case of Obsessive Neurosis' (1905 Coll. Papers III:363) Kanzer (1958:476) also speaks of

> 'elliptical thinking', a term applied by Freud to obsessive doubt about an immediate object in place of a repressed thought that cannot be spoken. The rejected thought is thus extruded as a projection; the conscious ideas that it links remain as an unbroken façade which, in the absence of apparent connections, may take the form of a delusion or be sensed as an inexplicable conviction, affect, impulse, inspiration, or bodily feeling attached to an idea.

4 Freud describes a holiday trip while travelling alongside a young man of his acquaintance, who was familiar with his work. The conversation led to his companion quoting

from a speech by Virgil in which Dido expresses her vengeful feelings for Aeneas, but he cannot quite get hold of the quotation and asks for Freud's help, which he is able to do, providing the correct quotation as, 'Exoriar(e) aliquis nostris ex ossibus ultor', noting that the elusive word is 'aliquis'. The man is curious to understand why he should have forgotten something that is in fact so familiar to him. Freud then takes him (and us) through a mini-analysis via the process of free association to which the young man somewhat embarrassedly submits as it becomes gradually clearer to him that the source of forgetting is related to anxiety concerning a pregnant lover and the unconscious wish for her period to miraculously appear.

5   We think of the mnemic residues as being contained in systems which are directly adjacent to the system Pcpt.-Cs., so that the cathexes of those residues can readily extend from within on to the elements of the latter system. We immediately think here of hallucinations, and of the fact that the most vivid memory is always distinguishable both from a hallucination and from an external perception; but it will also occur to us at once that when a memory is revived the cathexis remains in the mnemic system, whereas a hallucination, which is not distinguishable from a perception, can arise when the cathexis does not merely spread over from the memory-trace on to the Pcpt. element, but passes over to it entirely. Verbal residues are derived primarily from auditory perceptions, so that the system Pcs. has, as it were, a special sensory source. The visual components of word-presentations are secondary, acquired through reading, and may to begin with be left on one side; so may the motor images of words, which, except with deaf-mutes, play the part of auxiliary indications. In essence a word is after all the mnemic residue of a word that has been heard.

((19–20). From Freud, S. in The Ego and the Id (1923–1925), S.E., 19:1–66)

6 A term coined by the French analyst, Laforgue, in 1926.

Chapter 6

Visual reverie
The therapist's daydream

In *Learning from Experience*, Wilfred Bion (1962) asks, 'When the mother loves the infant what does she do it with?' and responds to himself that, 'Leaving aside the physical channels of communication my impression is that her love is expressed by reverie' (35).

I have been looking at the way in which the analyst's visual reverie indicates a form of internal communication – a dialogue that is taking place within – that may be provoked or stimulated by the patient or that may be a result of personal concerns that in some way relate to the patient. Additionally, the shift from verbal-thought to imagery may also indicate a defensive posture in relation to either of these or, conversely, it may suggest a move towards intuitive understanding that is temporarily otherwise inaccessible, thereby providing a path through a current impasse in the therapeutic process. As indicated earlier, I regard mental imagery as ubiquitous, persistent and continuous – even if often 'invisible', elusive, blurred or in some other way out of conscious awareness. Further, I regard the analyst's daydream – or visual reverie – within the clinical setting whether elusive, dreamily blurred or sharply focused, as equally persistent, but functioning in visual form much as the well-enough attuned mother's reverie does in relation to her infant. Here, I look more closely at the analyst's daydream, expanding further upon its function, and then illustrate some of these ideas with a variety of examples from clinical practice.

Daydream as processor of projections

In speaking earlier of projection and projective identification, the discussion was clearly not referring either to a conscious wish to communicate – or the wish to communicate something that is conscious – but rather the communication that takes place in spite of the communicator. While recognising that it is not clear precisely how the subject communicates and the object grasps the projection, we nonetheless, recognise that the object or recipient of the projection is somehow affected by it, so that, while not always either a sharp tool or a blunt instrument, it is undoubtedly a powerful one. Alongside the numerous subliminal clues and indicators through which projective processes are communicated, received and understood, I suggest that it may also be the visual elements of the reverie or daydream that may provide us with clues as to both the content and the function of the unconscious projection. The following descriptions of the therapists' construction and processing of their own images will help to illustrate and clarify these ideas.

Arlow considers the dominant role of vision generally in human perception and refers to what Bertram Lewin describes as 'the pictorial nature of the individual's store of memories' (Arlow 1969:49). He holds that some form of visualisation is taking place as the analyst attends to his patient's free associations, together searching for the 'picture' the patient has stored within.

> In a sense, we dream along with our patients, supplying at first data from our own store of images in order to objectify the patient's memory into some sort of picture. We then furnish this picture to the analysand who responds with further memories, associations, and fantasies; that is, we stimulate him to respond with a picture of his own. In this way the analyst's reconstruction comes to be composed more and more out of the materials presented by the patient until we finally get a picture that is trustworthy and in all essentials complete.
>
> (Arlow 1969:49)

While this is a description of a more direct and more conscious visual responsiveness than the form of visualisation with which I am primarily concerned, it is nevertheless, a broad, and I think, accurate, statement of the continuous and ubiquitous nature of mental imagery. Whatever the many modes it may take, whether concordant and empathic, anxious and defensive or hovering somewhere between the two, it refers to the characteristics of responsiveness and 'collaboration' or 'co-construction', in some form, in relation to image formation.

Wilfred Bion (1965) also emphasised the visual nature of unconscious fantasy, commenting that he often grasped his patient's meaning 'by virtue of an aesthetic rather than a scientific experience' (52), that is to say, one that was sensed, as much as thought, in line with the notion of the analyst's reverie, or daydream. However, whereas the term 'reverie' (as indicated in the 'Introduction', 'the therapist's internal reflection that takes place during the session while staying in affective touch with the patient') is recognised as an essential and powerful tool in the work of therapy, the term 'daydream', by contrast, is more often employed to describe a somewhat more informal, detached state, a 'break' or recess from the intensity of the session – although often attributed to boredom – where the work in hand is being avoided or evaded, and therefore, something to 'come out of' as soon as it is recognised. This tendency to describe what is taking place within the analyst as either 'reverie' on the one hand, or 'daydream' on the other, may also be to do with the fact that the daydream may be identified precisely as the form of reverie that often contains imagery that is not readily recognised as relevant, either due to the seemingly disconnected nature of the imagery itself or because the visual component is transformed rapidly – functionally or defensively, as described above – into lexical thought or actual spoken words, and the images evaporate, as may happen with a nocturnal dream.

Shared imagery

As described earlier (p. 60), Otto Isakower (1957, 1963), in seeking to devise a reliable technique in support of analytic training, brought together two related Freudian clinical observations: hypnagogic states and 'evenly suspended attention'[1] (Freud 1912:111), out of which he developed the concept of the 'analyzing instrument' as a clinical tool. Isakower takes this oscillation between lesser and greater states of consciousness as his model of the analyst's basic position, functioning as a more consciously reflective counterpart to the patient's ideally unconstrained free association. Intrigued by this distinctive mental state, he uses Freud's image of the analyst turning his own unconscious 'like a receptive organ towards the transmitting unconscious of the patient', and begins to extend the metaphor of the instrument further by systematically exploring these more regressive states within a mind that is at the same time functioning at a highly sophisticated level. He reiterates Freud's advice that the physician should, 'in a state of easy and partial attention … catch the drift of the patient's unconscious with his own unconscious' (Freud 1923:239).

I have referred earlier to Freud's remarks, in *The Interpretation of Dreams* (1900), on the differences in the mental state between the more intense internal reflection and the more relaxed psychological self-observation, the latter state being similar to that before falling asleep, and more readily admitting 'involuntary ideas' to emerge that take the form of visual and acoustic images (Freud 1900:102). Then, in Chapter 7 (ibid.), Freud refers to two sensory surfaces of consciousness: one surface directed towards perception and the other towards preconscious thought-processes (ibid.:574). Isakower regards these two sets of statements together as containing the nucleus of the 'analyzing instrument', which he considers the therapist's most versatile and effective tool, at once both fundamental and sophisticated. He notes how individual views begin to converge into a composite picture, comparing the form deliberately to musical counterpoint, using the term 'instrument' in both its technical, but also its musical sense, and emphasising the importance of the analyst's use of his sensual and imaginative faculties, including mental imagery. In describing how the two states oscillate and come together, he also adopts another technical metaphor, this time of a range-finder device that coalesces two separate images into sharper, and deeper, focus, noting that visual forms more readily accommodate themselves to 'blending into one formulation than do verbalized ones' (Isakower 1992:198), echoing Freud's remarks on dream construction (see Chapter 4, pp. 68–69) where he describes how the transformation of dream-thought into pictorial language both fulfils the numerous demands of the dream for camouflage, but also fulfils the demand for ideational economy. Isakower conveys a sense of the character of this experience, as 'rough tracings', or visual representations of the patient's material, juxtaposed with images that arise from within the therapist noting, 'You may even visualize the spelled out word before your inner literal eye ...'. Then, 'a transitory disintegration takes place, to be followed quickly by the necessary reintegration and we may see, like an "exploded view", the way things were "fitted together" ' (202–203). This description of jointly constructed images resonates with the ideas I set out earlier in relation to the 'day's residues', in which the patient's material may provide the catalyst for the therapist's day-dream, even when the two do not appear to be immediately linked. (See p. 106 for a striking example of this from Simon.)

Two decades on, Balter, Lothane and Spencer, Jr. (1980) revisit Isakower's (1963) work on the semi-hypnotic state he described in relation to both the free association of the patient and the 'analyzing instrument' of the analyst, and see it as inducing a state of mind ideally suited to heuristic enquiry and discovery. The authors draw attention to Ernst Kris's (1950) exploration of preconscious mental processes, describing the state of mind in which free association functions as one that induces a change in formal qualities of thought from logical formulation to dreamlike imagery as well as a regressive shift from secondary towards primary process thinking, and from ideas expressed verbally to those expressed in terms of images. As this condition coexists with the analyst's need to remain alert to the state of mind of the patient, the authors further develop the concept of the 'analyzing instrument', fluctuating between those more regressed, primary process states and the more alert, waking states, but where, in this space of oscil-lation, the analyst is usually 'more likely to perceive the connections between words, ideas and images which are products of the patient's primary process.' But further, due to the analyst's corresponding regressed state, 'the patient's words are more likely to evoke visual, auditory, and bodily images in the analyst' (Balter *et al.* 1980:491).

Just as becoming aware of the imagery, or the repeated imagery, in the patient's material would provide the therapist with the opportunity to observe, or to draw attention to the patient's defences or anxieties, so does gaining conscious awareness of her own visual ideas and images draw her attention to both her own, and possibly the patient's, defensive operations. Conversely, it may equally be true, that if the analyst usually experiences images while listening to the patient, and becomes accustomed to paying attention to this process, then absence of such imagery – experiencing only 'lexical' representations – may alert her to an altered level of relationship to the patient or his material.

Horowitz (1970) describes this process in the therapist who passively allows the formation of an image in relation to something described by the patient that generates empathic understanding, and a shared imagery that is held in common. He goes on to note, however, that the therapist's images are not always congru-ent with the patient's narrative, and while this could be a sign of lack of empathy, it may be equally connote something more constructive that may furnish the therapist with alternative ways of thinking about the patient's material – providing of course she is in a position or a frame of mind, to catch hold of it. If that is the case, then the internal image that arises in her mind may hold the 'kernel of an interpretation' that is not only true, but offers the possibility of a fresh articulation (292).

Thus, images can serve as guidelines or indicators, of the nature or character of feeling, particularly with regard to complicated affective states that are difficult to articulate verbally. This is especially so, as they tend to enter awareness spontaneously, and are less under conscious control, being part of a continuous, silent, unconscious or semi-conscious background, like the 'inner movie' described earlier that is invisible during the waking day, but comes more sharply into focus in the 'dark' and relative quiet of the hypnagogic state, in reveries, daydreams or dreams. The picture, however, becomes both more complex and more interesting as the clinical research into the phenomenon of the analyst's imagery develops.

James Kern (1978), for example, speaks of his gradual awareness of previously unnoticed visual images that arose spontaneously as he listened to his patient's associations, images which seemed unusual, first, in that he could discern no apparent connection either to the patient's material or to his conscious thoughts about the patient; and second, in relation to a striking discrepancy between the visualised foreground of the patient's speech or descriptions, and the background setting that the therapist provided for them, which were specific and detailed, rather as though the patient was responsible for the narrative, but the analyst was responsible for the setting. The analyst's images – usually banal but detailed background visualisations often exhibiting the characteristic of spatial constancy – took the form of landscapes, architectural features, houses, furnishings, room arrangements and so forth and tended to have a somewhat persistent, indelible quality. He came to understand that these images contained 'transferred fragments of conflictual early object relations and projected self-representations' (27) and were similar to screen memories, as described by Suler (1989) in that 'the image served a dual function: Its overt appearance enlightened him in his analytic work with his patient, whereas the seemingly inconsequential details in the "woodwork" of the image protected the repression of genetic material' (354). This description most closely describes my own experience, and perhaps accounts for the complexity in describing it, as it is somewhat like watching, and trying to focus on two films – or two versions of the same film – at once.

Clinical illustration: Ms. J

An example of this tendency to provide the 'setting' for the patient's narrative may be illustrated by a session with Ms. J, a young professional woman. She was a bit late for her session as a result of the last of a string of irritations and frustrations of the day. These began with starting off farther away than usual from our appointment, due to having attended a meeting some distance from her place of work, that hadn't gone well. The train she planned to take from the meeting to get to me had been cancelled, so she decided to take a bus as far as she could then walk the rest of the way. The bus was moving very slowly in traffic so she jumped out and caught a taxi. She suggested a short-cut to the driver, but this proved to be ill-advised, as a result of which she was now late, and now 'didn't know where to start' because all she could think about was how everything had gone wrong, and now there wasn't enough time to talk about anything.

I started off by following what she was saying, imagining her trying to get to her session, but found myself inexplicably placing her narrative (and, it gradually dawned on me, not for the first time) quite specifically in a part of town I recognised, but one that was unrelated in any way to her account. I could see this site, an intersection consisting of three roads, a side road and a bridge. In my mind's eye, the patient was standing at the main road of this intersection, with the bridge just to her left, the road that extended from the bridge to her right, a road at an angle diametric to this and the road straight ahead. It seemed that the bridge linked a more affluent to a more deprived neighbourhood. In my mind, Ms. J was standing motionless on the 'affluent' side of the junction, as if stopping at a red light, perhaps, waiting to cross. The scene in my mind was almost static, other than for sparse or slow-moving traffic. Interestingly, I could see this location as if from quite a high angle, which meant that I was aware of movement in all five directions, ahead of her, behind her, to the left, to the right and at an angle. I attached no significance to the specificity of the site; it seemed to be simply a setting I had for some reason provided for her narrative. I then began to notice that as Ms. J was speaking of the frustration of trying to get to me, in my image, she remained rooted to the spot, as if paralysed or unable to decide which way to go. The scene stayed in my mind's eye like a paused frame, rather than a moving image. In going over what she had been saying about the day's tribulations, I tried to think back to see if she had said something that brought this place to mind, but there was nothing I could recall that would specifically place her there. It was just a 'junction'.

Then the phrase, 'up the junction'[2] came to mind, a film, I remembered from the 1960s, controversial for its time, but I set that aside as a distraction. However, I then remembered – or thought I remembered – that one of the themes of the film was abortion, and I knew, as part of her history, that Ms. J had had an abortion when she was younger, although it had not figured consciously in any of her current difficulties or in the material of recent sessions. Although the matter of the termination had been discussed previously as a significant and unhappy event in her life, the patient was clear that it had not been at the time, nor was it now, an issue of conflict for her. But it occurred to me in this session that it was not just the abortion, but also the circumstances surrounding her life at the time – far more distressed and chaotic than at present – that might be involved. I wondered if perhaps we were speaking of being stuck at this junction, seemingly on the 'safe' side of the bridge, but in

Figure 6.1 'Junction: bridge and crossroads'.
Source: F. Carey.

sight of, and closely associated with the 'troubled' side. The image conveyed both a bridge and a crossroad and it seemed that the patient was trying, but was unable, to move – or move on – from any associations (the bridge) that connected her with that unhappy time. She could not have taken any of the paths available to her without encountering or in some way connecting with the bridge. In allowing to go unchallenged the idea that this aspect of her past was not an 'issue', I too seemed to be regarding the bridge as a barrier to be avoided, something to have 'got over', not something to 'go over', and see it for the link that it could provide towards enabling movement. I too seemed to be stuck at this junction.

I understood what my patient meant when she said that the conscious decision regarding the termination was unconflicted for her. It had been a difficult time, but she had never regretted the choice she had made as she was as certain now as she was then that she did not want a child at that time when she was very young and single. However, it was not easy to avoid the many associations to these events that were so central to both her past and present life. Thinking over her narrative, I considered that what she had been describing in speaking of the difficulty and frustration of her day, not being able to get where she wanted, feeling thwarted and blocked, feeling cut off from me, trying to find a 'short-cut' and so forth, may also have alluded to not being able to find her way to thinking about something difficult, without help. I think it was the image of the 'junction' that drew my attention both to the film, then the setting, the sad events that took place there where she felt abandoned, which prompted me to think more about how almost everything she did every day could serve as a reminder of what she wanted to forget, but could not. The image of the 'junction' prompted me to reconsider with her the importance of these events, in spite of her insistence that they were 'no longer significant'. Once again, this image was entirely my association to something that I may have been missing. Not hers.

Striking similarity of image

An unusual example of strikingly similar imagery between therapist and patient comes from Bennett Simon (1981) who develops the themes of empathy through imagery but, by contrast, also considers the possibility of non-verbal, imagistic experience signalling a difficulty in communication between analyst and patient. He writes of an instance of strikingly congruent imagery shared between analyst and patient during a session, that he ascribes to a state of deep, empathic communication between the two, where, however, the nature of that communication included elements of dissonance such that while remaining in touch through the imagistic level of communication, they were also individually engaged in autistic reverie, 'a meditation on loneliness' (471). It may be helpful to provide some of the content of the session to amplify these ideas in his work with this patient, a young man, a scientist, married with two young children.

Prior to the session in question, the patient 'P' had mistakenly cancelled two sessions, which the therapist could not then reinstate. P has just returned from a trip where he presented a paper at a conference. He spoke of the pleasure of a successful presentation, 'slightly marred by his competitive feelings'. On the return flight, he recounted an embarrassing incident where, flustered by the attractiveness of the stewardess, he clumsily reached for the drink she was offering to his neighbour, spilling it in his own lap.

Here, Simon starts to relate his own stream of thought as it begins to come to his notice while the patient is speaking. He sees the patient in the aeroplane:

> Lusting after the stewardess – spilling the drink ... fouling his own nest ... meetings with colleagues, rivalry — convention — I should write a paper I've been meaning to get together – expand my thoughts on the Odyssey, hero as an only child ... Odysseus' rivalries as sibling rivalries – his lies, one of his lying names, Aithon – 'firebrand' ... [this] is also the name of a bird, which in folklore, somehow everts its stomach and then eats it – good point for my thesis on oral aggression and sibling rivalry in the poem – arresting image [that] keeps coming (I envision a cormorant-like bird everting its stomach, as if through its belly button).

> (473)

At this point, the therapist snaps himself out of his daydream and says to P that he seems to have been unhinged by his attraction to the stewardess, to which P replied, that in fact what he was most upset about was missing the two sessions, then continues:

I have an image now of something I heard in a lecture on the black widow spider – the supreme sacrifice of the mother. She turns her stomach out and her own digestive juices start to eat away at her body so that the little spiders can eat her up.

(Ibid.)

Simon is understandably struck by the extraordinary similarity in the two images, although not a word has been spoken at any time in reference to either the bird or the spider. He also notes 'the interesting difference' between his image of the bird eating its stomach, and P's image of the spider digesting herself, which 'hit me like a thunderbolt' (ibid.). However, rather than share this with the patient, he waits to hear more. P is intrigued by the image of the spider associated to his feeling of loss. He regrets having needlessly 'sacrificed' his two sessions (Simon adds thereby 'stewing in his own juice', like the spider) and wishes that he could make more use of the therapy in his everyday life, 'translating' what happens in the consulting room to the world outside. The therapist responds, 'Perhaps you have been devaluing the analysis and thereby interfering with that translation.' P wondered if perhaps he had allowed himself to believe that he was in analysis for the sake of his children, behaving in a self-sacrificing manner like the spider, and not wanting them to suffer in the way that he had in relation to his dysfunctional father. The therapist wonders if perhaps P is in fact resentful at sacrificing himself for the sake of others. For Simon, the striking imagery of the session drew attention to the meaning of P's error in wrongly cancelling the two sessions, allowing him to become more immediately aware of the value of the analysis and that he had possibly been devaluing its importance due to unconscious resentment that he was doing this for the benefit of others. The images did not recur, and the therapist did not share the visual coincidence with his patient.

Returning to Kern's research on spontaneous imagery in the countertransference (1978), he is puzzled as to why he processes certain material by picturing it in this way, but with other clinical experience he works either non-visually or else pictures scenes more directly following the patient's prompts. Kern's research, based on the assumption that the imagery arises out of the empathic process, suggests that the backdrop nature of the overall visual content of the analyst's image may carry information about the presence and nature of the countertransference. He expands upon the detailed, specific and stable visual imagery that arises as the analyst listens, and suggests that this could represent a thwarted wish to retreat into sleep in order to avoid feelings provoked by the patient's material. In that case, the background detail in the analyst's imagery is a more conscious expression of the unconscious wish to retreat, but this visualisation allows the analyst to recognise what is happening as resistance. As with manifest-dream elements, or screen memories, it appears to be a form of camouflage that both conceals, but at the same time reveals the more significant, potentially uncomfortable, material. He writes:

Just as a neurotic symptom will maintain its structure over time ... so also does the backdrop element, a neurotic compromise in visual form, repeated over and over as a regular facet of the analyst's imagery. And, unless disrupted analytically, the backdrop element will persist as a stable screen-like form which expresses and disguises those impulses and defences which are stirred in the analyst's mind by the analytic material.

(Kern 1978:44)

He discusses the relationship of these ideas to the role of empathy, intuition, projection and introjection, including considerations of those regressive ego operations necessary to access empathic states, such as 'trial' fantasied psychic merging or sudden fantasying or daydreaming that seem to be part of, or essential to, this process.

Sympathetic and reciprocal identification

A variation on the experience described above of placing the patient's narrative in the therapist's own associative setting comes from James McLaughlin (1975) who speaks of the spectrum of attention, from that of extreme vigilance at one end to that of falling asleep at the other, which includes the state of altered consciousness brought about by freely-hovering attentiveness that includes reverie, dream and daydream. He notes that drowsiness in the analyst may reflect both his own personal conflicts as well as 'quite specific and dynamically appropriate counter-resistance and countertransference responses to his patient's conflicts' or a combination of the two (364). Apart from becoming useful tools in understanding both the patient and himself, these phenomena constitute defensive and expressive compromises, similar to those of the dream, and may provide the analyst with similarly rich clues with regard to unconscious material.

McLaughlin notes that his own capacity for visual imagery is activated mainly in states of reverie akin to dosing. However, he describes using a form of active imagination that enables him to be in affective touch with the patient as follows:

If he is, in dream or related incident, in a room or on a street, so am I. These sites are initially only vaguely perceived. Gradually his associations, past or present, usually permit the place or scene to be more specifically experienced in the context of what I know about them. I then can expect "runs" of ideational-affective content that concern other recent or historical data connected with the patient or occasionally with myself. When the latter trend becomes more than marginal, i.e., when idiosyncratic internal content begins to be so engrossing as to threaten to over-shadow the patient-centered content in my imagery, this fact must be noted and then suppressed for later self-inquiry.

(367)

McLaughlin classifies analytic response to the patient broadly into two categories, or two kinds of transient identifications: one is a sympathetic identification with the patient, in touch with his feelings, and the other is a reciprocal identification, in touch with the position of the patient's object, somewhat similar to Racker's (1957) use of the terms 'concordant' and 'complementary' identification with regard to countertransference, and also similar to what Bollas (1983) describes in writing on 'direct' and 'indirect' use of the countertransference. When these positions are challenged, the therapist may revert (temporarily, it is hoped) to any number of defences or regressive behaviours amongst which may be imaging or visualisation. McLaughlin suggests that such low-level motor activity helps to keep a balance between activity and passivity, alertness and drowsiness, which also functions to reduce tension. In such cases, imagery, particularly repetitive or compulsive imagery, may be an indication of such tension, and serve to alert the therapist to its existence, somewhat as I described earlier in relation to a visual 'fetish'.

As an example, he speaks of a supervision session in which the trainee felt drowsy while listening to his patient vaguely recounting an event that took place with other children in a back garden, when the analyst was suddenly startled into wakefulness by a vivid, visual, image of the patient's face as a clown, which seemed at the same time to be his own face. This recalled an event in his own childhood in which, he had been publicly humiliated by other children that he then linked to a shameful memory on the part of the patient. Here, the analyst's drowsiness appeared to be a defence against sympathetic identification with the patient's memory of humiliation, but the hypnagogic state then enabled a link to the feeling being defended against. He concludes with the observation that the more defensive or regressive reveries and daydreams often refer to past, present or anticipated situations in which the analyst felt or would feel safe, competent or fulfilled – once again, similar to the description above of the habitual or fetishistic type of daydream retreat – and often in areas unrelated to the therapist's psychoanalytic practice and identity, as if expressing the wish to be somewhere else (376).

This condition is often attributed to boredom, but it may be more a consequence of anxiety aroused by the patient (of which boredom may of course be a symptom). On the other hand, those daydreams or reveries that arise in more hypnagogic states are more likely to be the result of primary-process thinking, less guarded, less censored, more freely associative, more closely reflecting the inner life of the analyst and only remotely, McLaughlin suggests, the patient's immediate material (378–379). I am suggesting that such underlying imagery, when it becomes conscious, may reveal not only something of the nature of the anxiety taking place within the therapist in relation to the patient's material, but also the nature of the patient's object relations, as the vignette illustrates, including the relation to the self as object (much as described by Bollas, 1982). Often, however, it is only through the repeated persistence of particular images in relation to specific patients, that these eventually come to consciousness. These must then of course be scrutinised through the therapist's or analyst's usual counter-transference filters.

Self-preserving imagery

In a remarkable study filming analysts at work with more or less 'difficult' patients, Freedman (1997) considers the video evidence demonstrating the analyst's non-verbal reactions to the patient to discern the boundaries between empathy, and constructive and destructive forms of countertransference. He suggests that the capacity to be in empathic touch with the patient without being overwhelmed, requires a form of 'vicarious participation' that enables the analyst to create 'a parallel affective and imagistic scenario that resonates with the patient's, while sustaining a thin, permeable boundary between that evoked scenario and the intrusion of highly personal interferences' (82). This, Freedman suggests, requires the creation of representational space, and for such analytic listening, this is essential. This is, in effect, a self-preserving function of imagery within the analyst, a 'semi-permeable' space of containment that protects the therapist from being overwhelmed, while still managing to stay in touch with difficult, complex material.

Further clinical use of analyst's emerging imagery

Returning to the research undertaken by Ross and Kapp (1962, see p. 94) that appeared between Racker's second paper on countertransference (1957, op. cit.), and Isakower's and Lewin's researches on countertransference imagery, the authors discuss self-analysis of the countertransference using the technique of dream interpretation, but based on the therapists' analysis of their own personal visual associations to the patient's dreams. They note that up to 1954 the two most commonly agreed definitions of countertransference are either the analyst's unconscious reactions to the patient's transference or, alternatively, the analyst's unconscious transference to the patient. In their co-authored paper, they consider both. As well as the influence that Kanzer's (1958) ideas on image formation had on their thinking (see pp. 86–87) they also refer to a publication by Colby (1958:99–100) noting that patients' descriptions of dreams evoke parallel responses in the analyst, who explores these inwardly, using his own associations to his own visual images thereby aroused. This stimulated the authors to pay attention to the visual images that came to mind while listening with 'evenly suspended attention' specifically to patients' dream descriptions.

Putting a dream into words, they note, is an indication of the dream-work that has taken place, including secondary revision. However, the form in which the analyst conceptualises it is new; his visual images of the patient's verbal representations reflect the minds of both analyst and patient. The authors note the relevance of the distinctions between the conditions applying to the two participants. Although, significantly, the patient is encouraged to communicate his associations, while the analyst transforms his ideas silently into images, the latter is at the same time less resistant, and more able to use the images that arise spontaneously in relation to the patient's narrative for both self-analysis, and analysis of the patient's transference. The analyst may become suddenly aware of these images as the patient reports a dream (their research was carried out specifically in relation to the analyst's responses to dream imagery) or they may be vague, fleeting images on the edges of consciousness that can nonetheless, be captured and exploited for the benefit of the therapy.

The authors review earlier writing on the use of visual images as both resistance and communication, or what may be seen as forms of enactment (see Deutsch 1953; Lewin 1955). They maintain, however, that while visual imagery may be regarded as a resistance to verbalisation, or secondary-process communication, it is nonetheless more accessible to analysis than acting out. They draw attention to the value of creative imagination in the capacity for empathy, and suggest that the images that come to the mind of the analyst in response to the patient's narrative can be used for self-analysis, somewhat as Kanzer described free association to the patient's images. Thus, images would be seen as components of the analyst's unconscious, functioning in parallel to the unconscious activity of the patient's mind (bearing in mind that we are not speaking of conscious visual translations of verbal descriptions, but images that arise more spontaneously in a state of freely-hovering attention). Ross and Kapp conclude that their method for self-analysis of countertransference images provoked by the patient's dream descriptions provides further means of making the countertransference conscious and, therefore, useful for interpretation (656). And further, of significance to my argument, such self-analysis can be applied similarly to visual images that the analyst has in response to material other than dreams.

The first sketch

Returning now to the earlier sketches that first drew my attention to persistent associated imagery that I described in Chapter 1 (Figures 1.1 and 1.2, p. 11), these visualisations, both the interior and the floor plan, came to mind with this particular patient, Ms. A, with such frequency, that I occasionally had to remind myself that this really was something that was coming from my own 'picture store', my own experience, rather than something that she had described to me of her own living conditions. There is an entrance hall, and a long narrow corridor extending from it. Off this corridor, to the left, there is a combined living room and dining room, and just beyond the dining room a kitchen space. Off the right side of the corridor are two bedrooms, a bathroom and a study. Beyond the drawn space, if the living room door were open, I would be able to see through the windows on the far wall a small square, a road, and the river beyond (all vaguely visible in my imagination).

I was familiar with this space, and thinking about it, remembered that to my knowledge it had over time served several functions: a nursery; a studio; an office; a student residence; a family residence; and for periods of time an unused empty space. Relationships were made and ended there, children were born and raised there, and people studied and were creative, successful, failed and also suffered losses in that space. However, it was mainly a transitional or temporary space. No one remained there very long, and there was no particular continuity from one group of residents or users or from one function to another. It was a versatile space from which to 'move on', mostly used as its inhabitants passed from one phase of their lives to another.

When the image first became 'visible' to me, and for some time after, I had a clear sense that this was where Ms. A lived. I could easily picture her elsewhere if she was specifically describing somewhere (a theatre, a school, a holiday and so forth) but in the absence of specific descriptions to the contrary, this is where she lived in my mind. I could only picture her with her back to the long wall of the corridor, somewhere in the middle, from where she could see the doors to the other spaces, but would not – in my vision – enter. If she turned her head in one direction she could see the entrance hall, and in the other direction, the doors to the living spaces. When she spoke of others, I could picture them in this space, but inhabiting the rooms from which Ms. A appeared either to be excluded or to exclude herself. She seemed always to be in this corridor, on her own, standing outside the inhabited or functional spaces, uncertain which way to turn, or where to be. She hesitated to join the others, when others were there, for fear that she would not be seen, or, if seen, then ignored, even though this was – in my mind – her own space.

About a year or so after I first became aware of the image, it was with some surprise that I noticed during one of our sessions that the space had altered. It was similar, but it appeared to have expanded, so that I could see more easily into the various spaces, and Ms. A was not always only in the corridor. The space appeared to be more 'furnished'. The configuration of the rooms remained as in the original, but I now saw that Ms. A was using and moving through the spaces, opening or looking out of a window, entering and leaving, sometimes with someone else. She seemed, in this revised picture, to have got to know the space and recognised that it was hers to use and that it offered some possibilities.

Over time, this image has fluctuated between the more static, stilted, claustrophobic original and the more open, developed inter-relational space just described. When one or other of these images comes to my attention from time to time while I am with Ms. A, I consider that it may be suggesting the nature of her internal world at that moment, as I sense it, opening up or closing down. The picture seems to correlate with the idea of a more split or persecutory state, excluding herself (and pushing me away) on the one hand, or on the other, one that suggests a more integrated position, allowing herself to be curious about herself and the world around her (and allowing me in).

Summary

In this chapter, I have expanded on earlier ideas concerning visualisation and imagery, focusing now on the therapist's image-rich daydream, in relation to his or her clinical experience and technique. Imagery in the clinical setting can be complex, elusive and, at times, seemingly contradictory, since visualisation can provide both a refuge from verbal articulation of disturbing thoughts, but can also represent a source of anxiety where imagery provokes difficult associations. However, as images – rather like dreams – tend to be layered, complex and diffuse, often enough their meanings may remain sufficiently obscure to provide a temporary escape from harsh articulation, while at the same time hold the kernel of relevant associative ideas that relate broadly to the patient's internal world, and more specifically to their emotional state in the moment. I suggest that the therapist, in a state of daydream or reverie has, or can develop, a means of access to all these processes, and come to recognise and discern, and make use of, their therapeutic value. I have described and illustrated some of these processes and phenomena, in both their defensive as well as their more creative capacities.

I suggest that the more sensitive and familiar the therapist becomes with her pattern of visualisation, and the more aware she becomes of the nature and detail of the imagery of her daydream, the more likely she is to be able to utilise this often devalued component of reverie as an effective tool of clinical practice.

Notes

1 An editorial note in the published article (Freud 1912:111) indicates that Freud refers to a previous use of the phrase in the case history of 'Little Hans' (1909b), S.E., 10:23, 'though the wording there is slightly different. The present phrase occurs again later, in 'Two Encyclopaedia Articles' (1923a), S.E., 18:239'.
2 The film, Up the Junction, based on the novel by Nell Dunn, was made in 1968 and directed by Peter Collinson.

Chapter 7

Conclusion

My objective has been to explore the changing place and fate of imagery, and the visual element generally, in the theory and practice of psychoanalytic psychotherapy. In doing so, I have placed a particular emphasis on understanding the function and significance of the therapist's visual reverie or daydream, as part of the task of comprehending the internal world of the patient.

It is clear that the visual component has diminished since the earliest days of psychoanalysis. While it is self-evident that the most obvious reason for its relative devaluation has to do with the fact that we communicate ideas mainly through the written and spoken word (even when discussing images), I nevertheless, believe that this loss goes beyond the simple consequence of the dominance of language that is obviously essential for communication within both the session, specifically and the profession, generally. I argue that it is also due to unconscious dynamic processes that are often, although not exclusively, defensive and that this defensiveness may be linked to anxieties that are aroused by both imagery on the one hand, and by language on the other. While images may provide a form of retreat or escape from the precision of lexical thought, at the same time they may, by their very condensed nature, transport us into areas of uncomfortable associations we wish to avoid.

This tendency to gravitate 'naturally' towards imagistic thought, and then defensively to retreat from it, may generate a form of oscillation in the minds of both the patient and the therapist, between lexical and visual ideation over the course of a session, or with one mode or the other dominating across sessions over a period of time. I argue therefore, that image and thought tend to hold each other in a form of defensive-creative tension or balance, with one providing a potential refuge from the other when either threatens impingement.

I have tried to illustrate this process through discussing aspects of relevant theory and through the use of clinical illustrations. Technically, we may see evidence of anxious or defensive responses through the therapist's retreat to a daydream, in what appears to be a form of escape, but one that may ultimately provide a space of reflection leading to insight, in much the same way as discovered through the associative analysis of a dream, or thoughtful attention to the countertransference. It seems to me that within this dynamic model, imaging and visualisation – particularly in the therapist's state of 'free-floating attention' – take on some of the classically dynamic properties of actual dreams, particularly as outlined in Freud's theory of 'dream-work' (1900), an idea I have adapted to describe what I have been calling 'daydream-work' (only for the purposes of comparison, as no new terminology is needed) or the processes of unconsciously, or preconsciously, converting the patient's material (the equivalent of 'day's residues') into the therapist's imagery, towards eventual understanding.

Specifically, as with the dream, Freud's dream-work processes – condensation, displacement, overdetermination and secondary revision – that I describe and illustrate with clinical examples, are characterised broadly by distortion, and are further subjected to 'considerations of representability', or the capacity to be presented to the mind in a visual, figurative or imagistic form. I have suggested that there is an equivalent, or parallel, process in the daydream that takes place within the analytic session, or in the images that rise up spontaneously within the therapist in relation to – although not necessarily as a direct result of – the patient's material, as indicators either of the therapist's countertransference or at times, also to impediments to that process.

Spatiality and dimensionality

I have put forward the view that imaging and visualisation can be seen as significant elements and indicators of dimensionality and, as such, have a role to play in the analytic process. I support this argument on the basis of two psychological and emotional ideas: first, the development of a spatial dimension, and then the growth of unconscious communication, as expressed through projective processes. From my critical survey of various psychoanalytic approaches to the place of spatiality in psychological and emotional development, I have focused on the fundamental role played by a growing capacity to tolerate experience of desire, frustration, loss and absence in establishing a space for imaging, imagining or representing, the lost, absent or longed for object.

I have further reiterated the link between dimensionality, imagery and unconscious communication by next focusing on the relationship between spatiality and theories of projection, symbol-formation and the continuous and continuing oscillation between more primitive and more dimensionally developed positions. This process introduces a further element that, of unconscious communication through projective processes, and particularly of the special case of such processes as evidenced by the therapist's countertransference in the clinical setting.

Projection and projective identification have been discussed and critiqued in psychoanalytic discourse in breadth and depth over a substantial period of time, furnishing us with ample clinical evidence of the often forceful impact of this experience, without necessarily fully accounting for how it comes about, but which remains elusive and rooted in primitive experience. I have suggested that the capacity for unconscious imagery, which I later go on to describe in greater detail, may be at least one such generating factor of the phenomenon.

In next focusing upon the therapist's countertransference as a particular form of projection, I concentrate specifically on those visual or imagistic experiences where the relationship to the patient's material is indirect, arising equally from the therapist's store of images, providing her with associations that, upon reflection, can be seen to relate to the patient's internal state and object relations. I have argued that such imagery arising spontaneously in the mind of the therapist may offer fresh insights in situations where the force of the projections may otherwise create an obstacle to verbal articulation. This idea is reinforced by the likelihood that, under certain conditions, the image – being especially robust in the more hypnagogic or 'fuzzy' states – may be less susceptible to censorship, particularly as its form and therefore, its meaning in such states are ambiguous. I later, however, go on to show that by contrast, when the form of the image comes more sharply into focus, and is therefore, more conscious and less ambiguous, it can itself arouse anxiety and the reverse process may take place, with a retreat into secondary process and language.

In my critical overview of attitudes towards countertransference over time, evolving as it has from a form of unavoidable, but regrettable, nuisance to a fundamental tool, regarded by some as the 'touchstone', of analytic insight, I have emphasised the approach that regards it as a process that is largely co-constructed. Following Racker's (1953) distinction between concordant and complementary countertransference experiences, I have applied these distinctions to the therapist's countertransference imagery, and provided examples of how these versions are manifest within the visual material of a countertransference experience from published accounts, as well as from my own clinical work. In the example of Mr. C (p. 38), illustrating a form of complementary 'visual' countertransference, I demonstrated how a seemingly unrelated daydream image of youngsters smoking behind the bicycle shed stimulated my awareness of a form of 'identification with the aggressor', in opposition to the weaker individual. This image-based identification fostered a sharpened awareness of the patient's provocatively masochistic behaviour that served to perpetuate a strongly held position of self-righteous grievance that was a marked feature of the patient's relationships. In the second example (p. 41), illustrating a form of 'concordant' visual countertransference, Mrs. D's passive silence provoked in me an image of a hallway, a stairway, a cupboard, and a state of near breathlessness that seemed to reflect her own stifling paralysis when confronted with the memory of a frightening experience. In these examples, and others taken from published accounts in support of my claims, I have placed emphasis on the importance of the role of apparently innocuous thoughts or distractions on the therapist's part, especially those that come in imagistic form in a state of free-floating attention. I have also indicated, and provided examples to show, that the image is constructed from sources within both the therapist and the patient as exemplified, inter alia, by Sandler's concept of intrapsychic role-relationships that take the form, in the therapist, of what he calls 'free-floating responsiveness', and Bollas's (1983) notion of 'direct' and 'indirect' countertransference.

These ideas, concerned broadly with the concept of the co-construction of the therapist's countertransference, all underpin my argument for nurturing a capacity for observation and registration of the associative imagery generated through contact with the patient.

Considerations of representability

Through my critical review of the evolution of the place of the visual in psychoanalytic discourse, I describe how the centrality of the image ceded in both practice and theory to the primacy of the word, both practically, as necessitated by the use of language for communication both within, and beyond, the consulting room, but more pertinently, due to those psychodynamic processes that impact upon the therapist in the clinical setting. Having established in principle both the incidental and the dynamic rationale for the relative recession of the image, I describe the processes of image construction itself, particularly in hypnagogic or similar states such as may arise in the conditions of the analytic session on the part of both patient and therapist, as referenced in Freud (1900:101, 344), Bion (1988), Lewin (1968), Arlow (1969) and Kanzer (1958, 1980), but most notably as detailed in the work of Isakower (1938, 1957) whose substantial research on the subject, much of which is detailed in his concept of the 'analyzing instrument', principally informs this section. Analogous to Bion's concept of maternal reverie, I argue that the regression associated to this state similarly evokes more primitive modes of object relationship, engaging all the senses including an increased capacity for imaging, and also imagining, the material of the patient (although it will be understood that I am speaking of images that arise obliquely, not directly, as a result of the patient's material). I refer to contributions from a number of writers in support of this argument, such as Warren (1961) and Horowitz (1970) particularly with regard to the inclination towards primary process thinking in a mildly regressive state, and the tendency for painfully repressed memories to come to consciousness first as images and then as narrative. I note also the role played by the characteristic ambiguity of the visual image, as remarked upon by Freud (1900) that enables an initial reduction in censorship.

However, to reiterate the observation I described at the start of this conclusion, while I believe that images provide a form of retreat or escape from the precision of lexical thought, at the same time the very ambiguity that results from its characteristic capacity for multiple associations may lead the daydreamer to anxious association he or she may wish to avoid – as in Hamlet's sudden anxiety at the prospect of the fulfilment of his wish to sleep, '... perchance to dream!' – that leads to an oscillation between lexical and imagistic thinking, either within the session or across sessions over time. In this way, I have suggested how image and thought appear to hold each other in a form of defensive-creative tension or balance, with one providing a potential refuge from the other when either threatens impingement. I have provided a number of clinical examples demonstrating this process, from both my own practice – where images that began as innocuous, led almost imperceptibly towards ideas that I recognised were tinged with more disturbing associations – as well as that of others who have noted the significance of imagistic thinking in the hypnagogic state and who report similar ambiguities or fluctuations.

Staying with the dynamic character of daydreaming, I indicate those fluctuations of thinking within more or less conscious states, as being consistent with Freud's description of the movement between conscious and preconscious systems (Freud 1925:231). Due to the similarity between dreaming and other forms of imagistic experience, I posit a link between sleep-dream and daydream-type experiences that, concurring with Arlow (1969), for example, become visible to the observing analyst in a number of ways including imagery, figurative language and screen memories. In thus, establishing the correspondence between sleep-dreaming and daydreaming, I consider how image construction in hypnagogic states can be further understood by applying Freud's model of dream-work to daydreams, or what I have referred to as 'daydream-work', the key that both encrypts and decodes the daydream's meaning, in a manner similar to its function in dreams. These daydream-work processes that I described at the outset of this concluding chapter include 'considerations of representability', or the capacity for ideas to be presented in a visual, figurative or imagistic form. By detailing this process in the clinical setting, I endeavour to show how the patient's material impacts upon the therapist's daydream, assisting in the generation of its content in a manner similar to that provoked by the 'day's residues' upon the sleeping dream (Freud 1900). As the patient's material stimulates the therapist's personal store of imagery, the images that result may thus, be described as, at least partially, co-constructed, and I propose that the patient's material is to the therapist's daydream as the 'day's residues' are to the dream.

I illustrate this process with personal examples that observe the therapist's imagery, usually persistent in relation to work with the particular patient. By tracing a series of associations back to the sources of these images, I discover significant points of congruency with the experience of the patient. However, I further observe that this slightly hypnogogic visual experience on the part of the therapist is, as with dreams, commonplace and thereby, can feel inconsequential. For this reason, its relevance is often overlooked with regard to the work with the patient that is taking place at the moment.

I pursue in greater detail the complexity of material absorbed into the concept of 'representability' in order to emphasise the intricacy of those chains of associations between things, and the words used to represent them, and conversely, between words and the objects they represent. This process produces a wealth of associations, and an intricate network of images, ideas and references, that provides the rich store of possible meanings available to both dreams and daydreams, further necessitating scrutiny of any given image for related themes or ideas, towards potential understanding. With regard to the last of the dream-work processes that I discuss, that of 'secondary revision', I conclude that while this may take the form of a plausible interpretation, it may also be an attempt to rationalise something in the session that is not yet understood, either distorting the process or pre-empting deeper understanding.

I draw attention to the relationship of imaging, representability or figurability to Bion's (1962) concept of alpha-function that can be seen as a development of Freud's theory of the dream-work component of representability, and its connection to sense impressions relating to the construction of the daydream. In doing so, I suggest that both the process and function of the daydream – if not identical with reverie (in that reverie does not necessarily present itself in whole or in part through image) – are nonetheless, comparable and both are or may be, used to process otherwise incoherent 'data'. Further, I agree with the view, as expressed by both Sharpe (1937) and later Meltzer (1983) that recognises the analyst's reverie or daydream as functioning also within an aesthetic dimension linked to the sensual, linguistic and visual components that – from earliest experience – underpin meaning through form and dimensionality, and emphasise that this pre-verbal mode often takes the form of imagery prior to being transformed into communicable word-based language. This construct provides a model of what might be described as a 'crucible' function of imagery within the reverie or day-dream, whereby imaging offers both a refuge from thought or from something unthinkable, but also a medium through which thinking and thoughts may become once again possible.

I go on to discuss a further aspect of the role of the image in the clinical setting through the phenomenon of screen memory, whereby the image that is accessible, and acceptable to memory, masks another that is painfully avoided and so less available for interpretation. The 'screen memory' may be seen as an inversion of the ambiguity of imagery, whereby it is the very vividness of the camouflage image that serves to disguise or to distract from the even more uncomfortable, concealed memory or idea (p. 95).

Through such dynamics, it is possible to see that on the one hand, the ongoing oscillation between imagery and verbalisation can be understood as a refuge from explicit, articulated speech and, on the other, speech and verbalisation can be seen as a refuge from the more primitive and persistent states that may be aroused by imagery; then third, and most significantly, the imagistic daydream can also be seen to function as a form of 'crucible', in which apparently disparate or chaotic thoughts and ideas may be transformed into clinical insight and understanding, there to be tested with the patient. Further, I hope to have reinforced the understanding that mental images, whether those of the patient or the therapist may enable articulation of otherwise obscure or complex ideas, through the details of relationships of objects, structure, texture, shape, tone, movement, rhythm, pace, space and so forth that may be grasped visually in an immediate, singular form, as with the single surface of a painting.

Other defensive positions in relation to visualisation may include fantasies that remove the subject (in this case, the therapist) from the setting, projecting uncomfortable thoughts elsewhere, for example, (in the illustration provided by Ross and Kapp) where the therapist's imagistic associations brought him to recognition of avoidance of the erotic transference (p. 94), or my own memory of the playroom, for example, where I was able to come closer to the genuine, rather than the apparent, feeling of the patient who was beginning to confront his dread of both his mother's as well as his own mortality (p. 80).

I have in this way argued that imagery may provide a shelter from unwanted thoughts, but the form that shelter takes may then expose to a more focused scrutiny the very thoughts that are seeking cover. When the imagery appears in the form of the therapist's daydream or visual reverie, the images – when scanned and analysed through the same processes that are used to scrutinise the dream – can often be seen to yield up associations to experience that, through the patient's material, have a bearing on his emotional or psychological situation. The patient's material in this way relates to the therapist's daydream as the 'day's residues' relate to the dream in sleep. In the examples I have used to illustrate the construction of the therapist's daydream, I have focused on those instances where the imagery arises at an oblique angle to the material of the patient, and rarely involves visualisation directly connected to what is being said, but more, to what is being inwardly 'heard'. I provide examples from several published accounts, as well as from my own practice, to illustrate the parallels that I have shown that I believe exist between dream and daydream construction and analysis.

Summary

To summarise, I have drawn attention to the significance of the therapist's visual reverie or daydream, particularly in view of the devaluation of the visual within psychoanalytic theory and practice. I hope to have shown that this devaluation has a strong dynamic element that is often defensive. However, by virtue of their richness and complexity, associations linked to such imagery may itself arouse anxiety, setting up an oscillation between lexical and imagistic thinking. I argue therefore, that 'image-thought' and 'verbal-thought' tend to hold each other in a form of defensive-creative tension or balance, with one providing a potential refuge from the other when either threatens impingement. Within this dynamic model, and particularly with regard to considerations of representability, the therapist's imagery and visualisation – in the hypnagogic state – are constructed in a manner similar to that of the dream, with the patient's material acting upon the therapist as the day's residues provide the genesis of the dream in sleep.

I have further proposed that the therapist's sensitivity and familiarity with his own capacity for, and pattern of, visualisation, particularly as manifest in the imagery of the daydream or reverie that occurs during the session – a feature that is often obscured or ignored – may enhance sensitivity to the patient's internal world, processes and relationships, both to himself and to others. I have thus, attempted to capture or – if it has been lost – to recapture, the essence and function of that imagery with the intention of providing a further analytic tool, as I conclude it does, within psychoanalytic practice and theoretical understanding. But, further, coming to develop a capacity for image formation, and to notice, evaluate and value it when it appears, may also enrich the therapist's own experience, and enhance the creativity of the work they do with their patients.

References

Abraham, K. (1913). Restrictions and transformations of scoptophilia in psycho-neurotics. *Selected Papers on Psycho-Analysis*. London. Hogarth Press and the IP-A, 1949. 169–234. (Cited in Lewin, 1954).

Arlow, J. (1969). Fantasy, memory, and reality testing. *Psychoanalytic Quarterly* 38:28–51.

Bálint, A., and Bálint, M. (1939). On transference and counter-transference. *International Journal of Psychoanalysis*, 20:223–230.

Balint, M. (1957). *The doctor, his patient, and the illness*. New York: International Universities Press.

Balter, L., Lothane, Z., and Spencer, J.H., Jr. (1980). On the analyzing instrument. *Psychoanalytic Quarterly* 49:474–504.

Bassin, D. (1982). Woman's images of inner space: data towards expanded interpretive categories. *International Review of Psychoanalysis* 9:191–203.

Berman, L. (1949). Countertransferences and attitudes of the analyst in the therapeutic process. *Psychiatry* 12:159–166.

Bick, E. (1968). The experience of the skin in early object relations. *International Journal of Psychoanalysis* 49:484–486.

Bick, E. (1986). Further considerations on the function of the skin in early object relations: findings from infant observation integrated into child and adult analysis. *British Journal of Psychotherapy*, 2(4):292–299.

Bion, W.R. (1956). Development of schizophrenic thought. *International Journal of Psychoanalysis* 37:344–346.

Bion, W.R. (1959). Attacks on linking. *International Journal of Psychoanalysis* 40: 308–315. Reprinted in *Second Thoughts*, 93–109.

Bion, W.R. (1961). *Experiences in groups*. New York: Basic Books.

Bion, W.R. (1962). *Learning from experience*. Maresfield Reprints, London: Karnac Books (1984).

Bion, W.R. (1963). *Elements of psycho-analysis*. London: Heinemann.

Bion, W.R. (1965). *Transformations: change from learning to growth*. London: Heinemann.

Bion, W.R. (1970). *Attention and interpretation: a scientific approach to insight in psycho-Analysis and groups*. London: Tavistock.

Bion, W.R. (1988). Notes on memory and desire. In E. Bott Spillius (Ed.), *Melanie Klein Today*, vol. 2, 17–21. (Originally published 1967 in *The Psychoanalytic Forum*, 2: 272–273; 279–280).

Bollas, C. (1979). The transformational object. *International Journal of Psycho-Analysis* 60:97–107.

Bollas, C. (1982). On the relation to the self as an object. *International Journal of Psychoanalysis* 63:347–359.

Bollas, C. (1983). Expressive uses of the countertransference: notes to the patient from oneself. *Contemporary Psychoanalysis* 19:1–33.

Botella C., and Botella, S. (2005). *The work of psychic figurability*. D. Birksted-Breen (Ed.). London. The New Library of Psychoanalysis.

Breuer, J., and Freud, S. (1893). The psychotherapy of hysteria from Studies on hysteria. *S.E.*2 (1893–1895): *Studies on Hysteria*, 253–305.

Calvino, I. (1974 [1972]). *Invisible Cities*. Translated by W. Weaver. London: Secker & Warburg, 1974. (First published Giulio Einaudi, Italy, 1972.)

Carpy, D.V. (1989). Tolerating the countertransference: a mutative process. *International Journal of Psychoanalysis* 70:287–294.

Colby, K.M. (1958). *A sceptical psychoanalyst*. New York: Ronald Press, 99–100.

Cole, E.M. (1922) A few "don'ts" for beginners in the technique of psycho-analysis. *International Journal of Psychoanalysis* 3:44.

Deutsch, F. (1953). Instinctual drives and intersensory perceptions during the analytic procedure. *Drives, Affects, Behavior*, R.M. Loewenstein (Ed.). New York: International Universities Press, Inc. (Cited in Kanzer, 1958; Ross and Kapp, 1962).

Deutsch, H. (1934). 'Okkulte Vorgänge während der Psychoanalyse' (Hidden processes during psycho-analysis) *Imago*, 12. (Cited in Racker, 1957).

Fairbairn, W.R.D. (1944). Endopsychic structure considered in terms of object-relationships. In *Psychoanalytic Studies of the Personality*. London: Routledge and Kegan Paul (1952).

Feldman, M. (1997). Projective identification: the analyst's involvement. *International Journal of Psychoanalysis* 78:227–241.

Fenichel, O. (1938). Problems of psychoanalytic technique. *Psychoanalytic Quarterly* 7:421–442.

Ferenczi, S. (1927). Missbrauch der Assoziationsfreiheit. *Bausteine zur Psychoanalyse* II. Vienna: Int. Psa. Verlag, 41. (Cited by Racker, 1957).

Ferenczi, S. (1950). *Further contributions to the theory and technique of psychoanalysis*. New York: Basic Books (1952).

Fisher, C. (1956). Dreams, images, and perception—a study of unconscious-preconscious relationships. *Journal of the American Psychoanalytic Association* 4:5–48.

Fisher, C. (1957). A study of the preliminary stages of the construction of dreams and images. *Journal of the American Psychoanalytic Association* 5:5–60.

Fisher, J.V. (2007). Alpha-function and the imaging position: (unpublished paper presented at conference: *The Roots of Creativity*, University of Westminster and Freud Museum, July 2007).

Foulkes, D., and Fleisher, S. (1975). Mental activity in relaxed wakefulness. *Journal of Abnormal Psychology* 84:66–75. (Cited in Suler, 1989).

Foulkes, D., Spear, D.S., and Symonds, J.D. (1966). Individual differences in mental activity at sleep onset. *Journal of Abnormal Psychology* 71:280–286. (Cited in Suler, 1989).

Freedman, N. (1997). On receiving the patient's transference: the symbolizing and desymbolizing countertransference. *Journal of the American Psychoanalytic Association* 45:79–103.

Freud, S. (1891). *On aphasia*. Translated E. Stengel. New York: International Universities Press (1953).

Freud, S. (1893–1895). The psychotherapy of hysteria from *Studies on Hysteria. S.E.*, II:253–305 (1953).

Freud, S. (1895). Project for a scientific psychology. *S.E.*, I [Pre-Psycho-Analytic Publications and Unpublished Drafts, 281–391].

Freud, S. (1895b). In J. Breuer, and S. Freud, *Studies on Hysteria. S.E.*, II (1953).

Freud, S. (1897). Letter 751 extracts from the flies papers. *S.E.*, I (1886–1899): Pre-Psycho-Analytic Publications and Unpublished Drafts, 268–271.

Freud, S. (1899). Screen memories. *S.E.*, III:301–322 (1962). (Cited in Kern, 1978).

Freud, S. (1900). The interpretation of dreams. *S.E.*, 4 and 5:344. London: Hogarth Press.

Freud, S. (1901). The psychopathology of everyday life. *S.E.*, VI London: Hogarth Press, 1960. (Cited in Kern 1978).

Freud, S. (1905). Fragment of an analysis of a case of hysteria (1905 [1901]). *S.E.*, VII (1901–1905): A case of hysteria, three essays on sexuality and other works. 1–122.

Freud, S. (1910a). The future prospects of psycho-analytic therapy. *Collected Papers* 2, 289. London: Hogarth Press (1946).

Freud, S. (1910b). Letter from Sigmund Freud to C.G. Jung, February 2, 1910. In W. McGuire (Ed.), *The Freud/Jung letters: the correspondence between Sigmund Freud and C.G. Jung*, 1974, 291.

Freud, S. (1911). Letter from Sigmund Freud to C.G. Jung, December 31, 1911. In W. McGuire, (Ed.), *The Freud/Jung letters: the correspondence between Sigmund Freud and C.G. Jung*, 1974.

Freud, S. (1912). Recommendations to physicians practising psycho-analysis. *S.E.*, XII (1911–1913): The case of Schreber, papers on technique and other works. 109–120.

Freud, S. (1912b-2013). Totem and taboo. *S.E.*, XIII:82.

Freud, S. (1913a). An evidential dream. *S.E.,* XII:267–278.

Freud, S. (1913b). Letter from Freud to Ludwig Binswanger, February 20, 1913. *The Sigmund Freud-Ludwig Binswanger correspondence 1908–1938*:112–113.

Freud, S. (1915). Further recommendations on the technique of psycho-analysis. *S.E.*, XII.

Freud, S. (1915). The unconscious. *S.E.*, XIV (1914–1916): On the history of the Psycho-Analytic Movement, papers on metapsychology and other works. 159–215.

Freud, S. (1915–1917). Introductory lectures on psycho-analysis. *S.E.*, XV (Parts I and II):1–240.

Freud, S. (1917). Introductory lectures on psycho-analysis. *S.E., XVI* (Part III): 241–463.

Freud, S. (1919). The 'Uncanny'. *S.E.*, XVII (1917–1919): an infantile neurosis and other works. 217–256.

Freud, S. (1920). Beyond the pleasure principle. *S.E.*, XVIII:7–64.

Freud, S. (1923). The ego and the id. *S.E.*, XIX.

Freud, S. (1925). A note upon the 'mystic writing-pad'. *S.E.*, XIX:225–232.

Freud, S. (1926). Inhibitions, symptoms and anxiety. *S.E.*, XX:75–176.

Freud, S. (1927). Fetishism. *S.E.*, XX:147–158.

Freud, S. (1930). Civilization and its discontents. *S.E.,* XXI:57–145.

Freud, S. (1938) Findings, ideas, problems. *S.E.*, XXIII:299–300.

Glover, E. (1927a). Lectures on technique in psycho-analysis (Part 1). *International Journal of Psychoanalysis* 8:311–338.

Glover, E. (1927b). Lectures on technique in psycho-analysis (Part 2). *International Journal of Psychoanalysis* 8:486–520.

Greenson, R.R. (1974). Loving, hating and indifference towards the patient. *International Review of Psychoanalysis* 1:259–266.

Grinberg, L. (1962). On a specific aspect of countertransference due to the patient's projective identification. *International Journal of Psychoanalysis* 43:436–440.

Grotstein, J. (1981). *Splitting and projective identification.* New York: Aronson.

Grotstein, J.S. (1978). Inner space: its dimensions and coordinates. *International Journal of Psychoanalysis* 59:55–61.

Heimann, P. (1950). On counter-transference. *International Journal of Psychoanalysis,* 31: 81–84.

Hinshelwood, R.D. (1997). Catastrophe, objects and representation: three levels of interpretation. *British Journal of Psychotherapy* 13(3):307–317.

Horowitz, M.J. (1970). *Image formation and cognition.* New York: Meredith Corporation.

Horowitz, M.J. (1972). Modes of representation of thought. *Journal of the American Psychoanalytic Association* 20:793–819.

Humphrey, G. (1951). *Thinking: an introduction to experimental psychology.* New York: Wiley and Sons.

Isaacs, S. (1948). The nature and function of phantasy. *International Journal of Psycho-Analysis* 29:73–97.

Isakower, O. (1938). A contribution to the patho-psychology of phenomena associated with falling asleep. *International Journal of Psycho-Analysis* 19:331–345.

Isakower, O. (1957). Transcripts of the curriculum committee of the New York Psychoanalytic Institute as reprinted in H.M. Wyman, and S.M. Rittenberg (Eds.), *Journal of Clinical Psychoanalysis* 1:2 (1992).

Isakower, O. (1963). Teaching and conduct of the analytic process, Chapters 2–7. (From the General Faculty Meetings of the New York Psychoanalytic Institute). *The Journal of Clinical Psychoanalysis* 1:2 (1992).

Isakower, O. (1992). Chapter three: preliminary thoughts on the analyzing instrument: a faculty discussion—14 October, 1963. *Journal of Clinical Psychoanalysis* 1(2):195–199.

Jacobs, T.J. (1993). The inner experiences of the analyst: their contribution to the analytic process. *International Journal of Psychoanalysis* 74:7–14.

Jarrell, R. (1955). *Poetry and the age.* New York: Vintage Books.

Jones, E. (1916). The theory of symbolism. In *Papers on psycho-analysis.* London: Bailliere, Tindall and Cox, 1948.

Jung, C.G. (1959). *The archetypes and the collective unconscious.* New York. Pantheon.

Kanzer, M. (1958). Image formation during free association. *Psychoanalytic Quarterly* 27:465–484.

Kanzer, M. (1980). Visual communication in the psychoanalytic situation. *International Journal of Psycho-Analysis* 61:249–258.

Kern, J.W. (1978). Countertransference and spontaneous screens: an analyst studies his own visual images. *Journal of the American Psychoanalytic Association* 26:21–47. (Written 1974).

Kernberg, O. (1965). Notes on countertransference. *Journal of the American Psychoanalytic Association* 13:38–56.

Klein, M. (1929). Infantile anxiety situations reflected in a work of art and in the creative impulse. *International Journal of Psychoanalysis* 10:436–443.

Klein, M. (1930). The importance of symbol-formation in the development of the ego. *International Journal of Psychoanalysis* 11:24–39.

Klein, M. (1946). Notes on some schizoid mechanisms. *International Journal of Psychoanalysis* 37:344–346.

Kris, E. (1950). On preconscious mental processes. *Psychoanalytic Quarterly* 19:540–560. (Cited in Balter *et al.* 1980).

Kris, E. (1953). *Psychoanalytic explorations in art*. London: George Allen & Unwin.

Kubie, L.S. (1943). The use of induced hypnagogic reveries in the recovery of repressed amnesic data. *Bulletin of the Menninger Clinic* 7:172–182.

Laforgue. (1926). In E.P. Farrow, 'Eine Kindheitserinnerung aus dem 6. Lebensmonat', *Int. Z. Psychoan.* 12:79, 280.

Laplanche, J. (2002). Après-coup. In A. de Mijolla (Ed.), *Dictionnaire international de la psychanalyse*. Paris: Calmann-Levy.

Laplanche, J., and Pontalis, J.B. (1973). *The language of psychoanalysis*. London: Hogarth Press.

Lasky, R. (2002). Countertransference and the analytic instrument. *Psychoanalytic Psychology* 19:65–94.

Lewin, B. (1946). Sleep, the mouth, and the dream screen. *Psychoanalytic Quarterly* 15:419–434.

Lewin, B.D. (1955). Dream psychology and the analytic situation. *Psychoanalytic Quarterly* 24:169–199.

Lewin, B.D. (1968). *The image and the past*. New York: International Universities Press, Inc.

Little, M. (1951). Counter-transference and the patient's response to it. *International Journal of Psychoanalysis* 32:32–40.

Masson, J.M. (1985). *The complete letters of Sigmund Freud to Wilhelm Fliess 1887–1904*. Harvard. Belknap.

McLaughlin, J.T. (1975). The sleepy analyst: some observations on states of consciousness in the analyst at work. *Journal of the American Psychoanalytic Association* 23:363–382.

Meltzer, D. (1966) The relation of anal masturbation to projective identification. *International Journal of Psychoanalysis* 47:335–342.

Meltzer, D. (1975a). *Explorations in autism*. D. Meltzer (Ed.). London: Clunie Press.

Meltzer, D. (1975b). Adhesive identification. *Contemporary Psychoanalysis* 11:289–310.

Meltzer, D. (1975c) Dimensionality in mental functioning. In D. Meltzer (Ed.), *Explorations in autism*. London: Clunie Press, 223–238.

Meltzer, D. (1983). *Dream-life*. Clunie Press for Roland Harris Education Trust.

Meltzer, D. (1992). *The claustrum: an investigation of claustrophobic phenomena*. London: Clunie Press.

Meltzer, D., and Williams, M.H. (1988). *The apprehension of beauty*. D. Meltzer (Ed.). London: Clunie Press.

Milner, M. (1952). Aspects of symbolism in comprehension of the not-self. *International Journal of Psychoanalysis* 33:181–194.

Milner, M. (1969). *The hands of the living God*. (and Virago Press, 1989).

Money-Kyrle, R.E. (1956). Normal counter-transference and some of its deviations. *International Journal of Psychoanalysis* 37:360–366.

Money-Kyrle, R.E. (1968). Cognitive development. *International Journal of Psychoanalysis* 49:691–698.

Ogden, T.H. (1979). On projective identification. *International Journal of Psychoanalysis* 60:357–373.

Ogden, T.H. (1985). On potential space. *International Journal of Psychoanalysis* 66:129–141.

Ogden, T.H. (1989). On the concept of an autistic-contiguous position. *International Journal of Psychoanalysis* 70:127–140.

Ogden, T.H. (1994). The analytic third: working with intersubjective clinical facts. *International Journal of Psychoanalysis* 75:3–19.

Ogden, T.H. (1997a). Reverie and interpretation. *Psychoanalytic Quarterly* 66:567–595.

Ogden, T.H. (1997b). Reverie and metaphor: some thoughts on how I work as a psychoanalyst. *International Journal of Psycho-Analysis* 78:719–732.

Olson, N. (2000). Pictures into words: visual models and data in psychoanalysis. *Psychoanalytic Study of the Child* 55:371–399.

Paivio, A. (1969). Mental imagery in associative learning and memory. *Psychological Review* 76:241–260 (as cited in Horowitz, 1970).

Phillips, S.H. (2002). The overstimulation of everyday life: II. Male homosexuality, countertransference, and psychoanalytic treatment. *Annual of Psychoanalysis* 30:131–145.

Piaget, J. (1945). *La formation du symbole chez l'enfant Neuchâtel* (Translation: *Play, dreams and imitation in childhood.* New York: Norton, 1962).

Racker, H. (1953). A contribution to the problem of counter-transference. *International Journal of Psychoanalysis* 34:313–324 (based on lecture delivered to Argentine Psycho-Analytic Association, September 1948).

Racker, H. (1957). The meanings and uses of countertransference. *Psychoanalytic Quarterly* 26:303–357.

Racker, H. (1958). Classical and present technique in psycho-analysis. In H. Racker (Ed.), *Transference and countertransference*. London: Hogarth Press, 1968, 23–70.

Rapaport, D. (1951). *The organization and pathology of thought.* New York: Columbia University Press.

Reich, A. (1951). On counter-transference. *International Journal of Psychoanalysis*, 32:25–31.

Reich, W. (1933). *Character-analysis.* New York: Orgone Institute Press, 1945, 4ff., 119–140.

Rosenfeld, H. (1987). Projective identification in clinical practice. In *Impasse and Interpretation*. London and New York: Routledge, 1987, 157–190.

Ross, W.D., and Kapp, F.T. (1962). A technique for self-analysis of countertransference—use of the psychoanalyst's visual images in response to patient's dreams. *Journal of the American Psychoanalytic Association* 10:643–657.

Sandler, J. (1976). Countertransference and role-responsiveness (written 1974) *International Review of Psychoanalysis* 3:43–47.

Schilder, P. (1935). Psycho-analysis of space. *International Journal of Psycho-Analysis* 16:274–295.

Searles, H. (1963). Transference psychosis in the psychotherapy of schizophrenia. In *Collected papers on schizophrenia and related subjects*. New York: International University Press, 1965.

Segal, H. (1974). *Introduction to the work of Melanie Klein.* New York: Basic Books.

Sharpe, E. (1937). *Dream analysis.* London: Hogarth Press. (Reprinted 1978 by Karnac, Maresfield Library).

Sharpe, E. (1947). The psycho-analyst. *International Journal Psycho-Analysis* 28:1–6.

Simon, B. (1981). Confluence of visual image between patient and analyst: communication of failed communication. *Psychoanalytic Inquiry* 1:471–488.

Spezzano, C. (2001). How is the analyst supposed to know?. *Contemporary Psycho-analysis* 37:551–570.

Spitz, R. (1956). Countertransference—comments on its varying role in the analytic situation. *Journal of the American Psychoanalytic Association* 4:256–265.

Spitz, R. (1965). *The first year of life*. New York: International University Press.

Stewart, H. (1985). Changes in the experience of inner space. *International Journal of Psychoanalysis* 66:255–264.

Suler, J.R. (1989). Mental imagery in psychoanalytic treatment. *Psychoanalytic Psychology* 6:343–366.

Tuckett, D. (1995). Mutual enactment in the psychoanalytic situation. (Unpublished MS.)

Tustin, F. (1980). Autistic objects. *International Journal of Psychoanalysis* 7:27–40.

Tustin, F. (1984). Autistic shapes. *International Journal of Psychoanalysis* 11:279–290.

Viderman, S. (1974). Interpretation in the analytical space. *International Review of Psycho-Analysis* 1:467–480.

Vogel, G., Foulkes, D., and Trossman, H. (1966). Ego functions and daydreams during sleep onset. *Archives of General Psychiatry* 14:238–248. (Cited in Suler, 1989).

Warren, M. (1961). The significance of visual images during the analytic session. *Journal of the American Psychoanalytic Association* 9:504–518.

Winnicott, D.W. (1949). Hate in the counter-transference. *International Journal Psycho-Analysis* 30:69–74.

Winnicott, D.W. (1953). Transitional objects and transitional phenomena—a study of the first not-me possession. *International Journal of Psychoanalysis* 34:89–97.

Winnicott, D.W. (1965). The maturational processes and the facilitating environment: studies in the theory of emotional development. *The International Psycho-Analytical Library* 64:1–276.

Winnicott, D.W. (1967). The location of cultural experience. *International Journal of Psychoanalysis* 48:368–372.

Winnicott, D.W. (1968). Playing: its theoretical status in the clinical situation. *International Journal of Psychoanalysis* 49:591–599.

Winnicott, D.W. (1971). *Playing and reality*. London: Tavistock Publications.

Winnicott, D.W. (1974). Fear of breakdown. *International Review of Psychoanalysis.* 1:103–107.

Winnicott, D.W. (1986) *Holding and interpretation. The International Psycho-Analytical Library* 115:1–194.

Wolstein, B. (1975). Countertransference: the psychoanalyst's shared experience and inquiry with his patient. *Journal of the Academy of Psychoanalysis* 3:77–89.

Index

Page numbers in *italics* denote figures.